LOW COST

Pole
Building
Construction

ENLARGED EDITION

LOW COST

Pole Building Construction

By Doug Merrilees & Evelyn Loveday

GARDEN WAY PUBLISHING

Library of Congress Catalog Card Number: 74-12663

International Standard Book Number: 0-88266-076-4 (paper)
0-88266-077-2 (cloth)

GARDEN WAY PUBLISHING, CHARLOTTE, VERMONT 05445

PRINTED IN THE UNITED STATES OF AMERICA

Book design by Sidney Solomon

CONTENTS

PART ONE

What You Need to Know About Pole Construction

Advantages of Pole Construction

Many people are becoming interested in pole building construction because they have heard or read that it is relatively cheap and simple. It is, but to understand exactly what it's all about, we should start with a definition:

Pole construction is building in which the vertical, load-bearing members are poles embedded in the ground, and which must be long enough to support the roof. The diameter of the poles usually is about six inches at the top ends, and they are spaced much further apart than are the uprights in conventional frame construction. No excavation is necessary beyond digging holes for the poles, and there is no concrete or block foundation. The poles serve the triple function of foundation, bracing and framework, to which the floor (if any), walls and roof all are fastened.

Labor, time and materials all are saved in the pole framing method. Since lateral girts replace the conventional wall studs, and since fewer and longer pieces of lumber are used, the actual framework of the building can be completed quickly. This is a real advantage in bad weather, as the project can be placed under cover rapidly.

Pole buildings have been approved where light frame structures are prohibited because of fire hazard. Pole framing members are so widely separated that fire is unlikely to spread from one to the other. Pole construction is now recognized by all four U.S. model building codes.

Other advantages of pole construction are: It is relatively simple to build, and little sawing is necessary. No scaffolding or forms are required during construction, and a minimum of construction labor is needed. In buildings where the loads are relatively light or the spans rather short, lower (hence cheaper) grades of lumber may be used. If the pole holes are dug by hand, only simple hand tools—the kind found in almost any household—are needed.

There are further advantages to this kind of construction in that round timbers have two distinct advantages from the standpoint of strength.

A circular timber is 18 per cent stronger in bending resistance than a rectangular timber of similar grade. A round timber, in practically all cases, possesses a very high proportion of the basic strength of its species. This is because the knots have only half the limiting effect on strength in the natural, round timber form that they do in sawed sections. Tests have shown that full-size round timber poles develop practically the full bending strength of clear wood.

Another advantage of pole frame construction is its high resistance to wind forces, which results because the poles that support the building are firmly anchored in the ground.

Later in this book general basic directions are given on how to construct a pole building, and these are followed by some specific plans. Right now it's enough to say that the poles are embedded in the ground, and they must be plumb.

The design of any pole building can be simple enough for unskilled persons to construct. Except for very small buildings, the step of setting the poles, however, is not a project for one person, the reason being that you have only two hands. For this step probably you should hire some

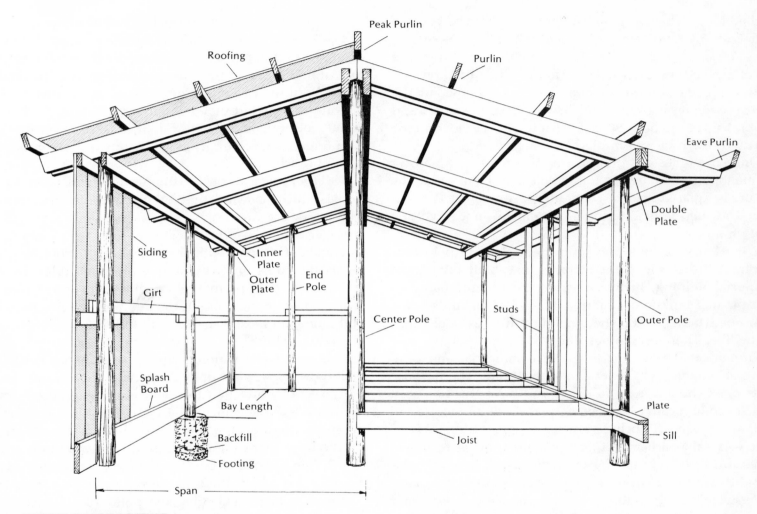

HOW IT GOES TOGETHER

Left side of this cutaway view shows embedment of poles, attachment of rafter plates, rafters, purlins and roofing. Below are the splashboards, girts and siding. The right side is for a more finished building, as indicated by floor plate and joists and wall framing inside the poles. Eaves are given more overhang.

unskilled help, which you will supervise, or maybe you can find neighborly help, or rent a machine to lift the poles.

In *Vermont Life* Magazine (Summer 1956 issue) there's a story of a pole-type barn-raising after a man's barn burned and his cattle were without shelter. Neighbors helped on the barn (the women cooked), and in two days the poles and main timbers of the new, 80-cow barn were secured, and the majority of the roof was in place.

Once the poles are plumb, the next step is to nail (or bolt) the longitudinal beams to the poles, and make sure the structure is squared up. The roof rafters are connected to this frame, and then your exterior is completed—not forgetting to put on a roof!

What kinds of buildings lend themselves to pole construction? The list is long and includes just about any type of commercial building, such as a warehouse or light manufacturing plant. Then there are farm buildings of all kinds—cow barns, horse barns, cattle sheds, poultry houses, tool sheds and the like. There are homes, too.

Prefabricated pole buildings for commercial and farm use are obtainable from several manufacturers. The purpose of this book, however, is to show you how you can do it yourself economically. Later some plans will be pictured in detail, and these will include houses.

It was said earlier that pole construction is relatively simple, but bear in mind the operative word here is "relatively." It would be cheating to give the impression it is as simple as making a sandbox for your youngster. But neither is it nearly as difficult (or expensive) as the conventional type of construction, which requires skilled labor, the extensive use of power tools, and more and costlier materials.

Pole building in varying forms is an age-old type of construction that dates back to the Stone Age.

Amos Rapoport in *House Form and Culture* says "There are cases where a way of life may lead to . . . a dwelling form related to economic activity rather than climate. For example, the Hidatsa of the Missouri valley were agriculturists from April to November, growing corn, greens and beans. During that period they lived in circular wooden houses 30 to 40 feet in diameter with 5-foot walls made of tree trunks and four central columns 14 feet high supporting rafters carrying branches."

Rapoport goes on to comment on resistance to lateral forces, such as wind or earthquakes, that requires either rigidity or bracing.

"The Fiji islands provide a number of examples of methods of dealing with the lateral force problem. In some areas the roofs are very simple and supported by central poles as well as peripheral columns. Since these poles are buried deep in the ground, the building acts as a rigid frame, although the flexibility of the members themselves assures some flexibility."

In pole construction the poles actually have an inherent ability to resist wind uplift, especially if the roof framing is very securely attached to them. In areas where hurricanes are expected, the value of this large resistence to uplift that is a part of pole construction should be considered seriously.

Why is there so much current interest in pole construction? There seems to be a batch of good reasons:

1. A limited amount of grading is required, and no excavation beyond digging the pole holes. Thus it can be accomplished without butchering the immediate area, and with a minimum disturbance of the natural surroundings such as tree roots and top soil.

2. Pole construction offers a way to lower building costs by utilizing, if desired, steep hillside locations which

present many problems for more conventional construction. There are no delays, either, in waiting for cement foundations to cure, for there are none.

3. As inflation causes the costs of building materials and labor to climb, there is a very real need for many people to find ways to build more cheaply than before. Pole methods allow such savings.

4. Ever since World War II there has been an ever-increasing interest in self-help. Not only are there many practical advantages to "doing it yourself," but there is a very tangible glow of pride and satisfaction when one completes his own project.

5. With the back-to-the-land movement increasing every year, many people are rejecting expensive and conspicuous life styles. They want and have only the simple tools for living, and are choosing to live in many ways as their ancestors did.

All of this adds up to the reason why pole construction may be the very thing to plan on, whether it is for a home or some other building that you need.

Very little has been published to date on pole construction. In fact it has been said that "the literature is non-existent." This is not quite true, for there are some few publications by wood products associations, which have been consulted here, and which are listed in the references at the back of this book.

The modern use of treated poles in the construction of restaurants, churches, schools, vacation cottages and homes began quite recently and as a West Coast phenomenon, gaining impetus with the construction in 1958 of a pole residence in California. Modern methods were learned through the experience of utility and outdoor advertising companies. At the time there was resistance both from lending sources and

NATIVE PERUVIAN POLE HOUSE

building code reviewers, but since then enthusiasm for the many advantages of pole construction has mushroomed.

The Poles Themselves

It's a well known fact that wood deteriorates because of bacteria, insects, fungi and dampness, and to delay such deterioration utility poles and fence posts have long been treated with preservatives. Companies which sell these and poles used in pole buildings strip the bark and then spray them with fungicides, which inhibit the attack of micro-organisms. Then the poles are pressure-impregnated with one of several preservatives.

Such poles can be purchased rather inexpensively, or if you have suitable trees on your own land which can be cut into poles, you can surface-treat them yourself, or better, find a place (inquire at lumber yards) where they can be pressure-treated.

Soft woods are favored for treated poles because they are porous and accept preservatives better than do the hard woods. Also they are easier to work with in terms of nailing or sawing.

Woods listed as approved for poles to be treated include Western larch, Southern yellow pine, Pacific Coast Douglas fir, lodgepole pine, jack pine, red or Norway pine, ponderosa pine, Western red cedar and Northern white cedar. White pine also is used in the East, as are white and red spruce.

However, if you have a ready access to white or red cedar, locust, redwood heart or cypress, the poles made from these woods will be inherently resistant to rot and micro-organisms. Hemlock also is rot-resistant but is more often used as lumber. These woods need not be pressure-treated, but should have the bark removed.

How long will poles last before deteriorating? This is important, since the poles are the foundation and strength of the structure.

There are varying answers. One firm which manufactures treated poles says: "In the Thirties a well-treated pole was supposed to last 30 years. Now this estimate has risen to 45 to 50 years, since anticipated failures did not occur. The length of service has been achieved under the most severe

conditions. Of course, any pole which you use inside your building will be protected, and an even longer life can be expected."

The American Wood Preservers Institute, conducting research for the Department of Housing and Urban Development, prepared the booklet *FHA Pole House Construction*, which sets forth guidelines acceptable to FHA for the construction of pole houses.

The AWPI is a non-profit organization doing research on pressure-treated woods of all kinds for all uses. Their comments on the durability of poles are especially valuable, although their standards are so high that not all manufacturers fully meet them.

AWPI says: "A house erected on poles produced for this purpose, and conforming to the rigid standards described below, is considered permanent—as permanent as a house on a well-constructed concrete foundation. The permanence is achieved by treating the poles with preservative. Using the newly-perfected 'assay method', pole manufacturers now can verify the adequate distribution of preservative in the finished product."

The assay testing method takes borings from the treated poles and subjects them to chemical analysis to determine the amount of preservative present.

AWPI goes on to say that "Users can be assured of the physical and preservative characteristics of the poles if the manufacturer indicates conformance with the AWPI quality control standards by the application of a permanent seal to each pole."

Although all the preservative treatments have their uses in pole construction, cleanliness, paintability, color and odor will determine the selection for a particular project. The methods are:

Water-borne salt preservatives: They provide clean, odorless, paintable, non-irritating pressure-treated lumber. For poles placed in the ground and subject to leaching, one should be sure to have that treatment which is chemically-bound—not that which is leachable. Recommended by the American Society of Civil Engineers are amoniacal copper arsenite, chromated copper arsenate or chromated zinc arsenate.

Pentachlorophenol in light petroleum solvent: The pole surface is comparatively clean and usually can be painted, provided the wood preserver knows prior to treatment that this is desired. There may be a slight odor until the petroleum has vaporized. This treatment has little effect on the color of the wood.

Pentachlorophenol in volatile petroleum solvent (gas-borne treatment): The wood surface also is clean, paintable and odorless, with its color that of the natural wood prior to treatment.

Creosote: The color varies from dark brown to black and the surface often is oily, especially when subjected to higher temperatures. Successful painting is impossible. These factors, plus the creosote odor, make these poles more suitable for use on the exterior of pole buildings. It should be noted that vegetation in direct contact with these poles will be killed for a year or two. Poles so treated are widely used throughout the United States by utility companies and are readily available.

Pentachlorophenol in heavy oil: The pole often has an oily surface, particularly when high temperatures cause an expansion of the liquid petroleum. Pole varies in color from light to dark brown, and an odor usually is present for a period of time. It is often difficult, if not impossible, to paint these poles successfully. Poles treated with this preservative also are readily available, since this too is a common treatment for utility use.

Preservative oils, creosote and the liquid pentachlorophenol petroleum solutions used on poles sometimes travel from the treated wood along nails, and will discolor adjacent plaster or finished flooring. Oil types, however, have a maximum service life.

Tar solutions applied to poles do not penetrate and preserve the wood. The protection offered, is temporary.

Cuts, such as notches or holes drilled through the preservative zone, should receive several liberal applications of wood preservative to retain the chemical integrity of the pole.

Home-Treatment of Poles and Skirting

Home builders who are unable to secure pressure-treated poles and skirting boards or find the costs prohibitive, can treat poles themselves using one of the newer methods developed at the U.S. Forest Products Laboratory.

The processes consist of soaking the green, undried wood first in one chemical solution and then in a second one. The two chemicals diffuse into the wet wood and then react with each other to form a compound that is poisonous to termites and to the fungi which cause rot. Moreover, the bonded chemicals are practically insoluable in water, and therefore do not leach out to any appreciable extent when the poles are used in moist soils. Some species of wood are more receptive to this treatment method (see page 12), and tests show that hardwoods are less receptive than the soft-woods as a class.

Several combinations of chemicals may be used in this home-treatment process, but the instructions given here employ materials more commonly stocked by chemical dealers.

About 25 pounds of technical (industrial grade) copper sulphate will be needed to treat 10 posts of average size, together with about 12½ pounds of technical sodium fluoride. Local farm supply and hardware stores may have to order for you from chemical supply houses, and the costs will vary according to quantity needed and shipping distances.

Because the solutions used here are harmful, great care should be exercised in handling the dry powders and the dissolved chemicals too. When working with the materials it is best to use goggles, rubber gloves and to avoid breathing the poisonous vapors and dust. If the chemicals should get on the skin or eyes, they should be washed out quickly. Clothes that are splashed by the chemicals should be rinsed in clear water and not washed with other clothing.

Treatment of your poles should start as soon as possible after they are cut—preferably within a week, or they will be too dry to accept the chemicals effectively. After cutting, pile the poles as closely as possible together and if available cover with a tarpaulin. Just before they are placed in the solution the poles should be trimmed six inches at each end and peeled of bark.

Preparation of the Solutions

The chemicals can be weighed out or measured in a one-pound size coffee can, which will hold about two pounds of chemicals.

The containers or pits (see illustrations) will be needed, one to hold each of the separate solutions. Copper sulphate is corrosive to iron, so if a drum is used it should be coated inside with pitch (heavy roofing tar) or lined with heavy polyethylene film.

The sodium fluoride solution is prepared in a proportion of three gallons of water to one pound of the chemical. The amount needed will depend upon the size of the container or pit used. Stir the solution well. Place the poles—as many as can be conveniently fitted into the container or pit—and add the solution to cover. Leave them to soak for three days.

Prepare the second container or pit with a solution of copper sulphate which has been mixed in the same proportions. Remove the poles from the sodium fluoride, using care in handling, and place similarly in the copper solphate container. Soak them there three more days and remove.

Meanwhile if more poles are to be treated, they can be started in the sodium fluoride pit, more of that solution being added to bring the level high enough to cover the poles.

The finished poles then should be rinsed in water so that they can be handled safely without gloves. Although they may be used at once in construction, it is better to pile them closely together for several weeks so that they will dry out slowly. This "rest" period helps to distribute the chemicals more evenly throughout the poles.

To dispose of the remaining chemical solutions, dump them in an open hole a safe distance from any wells or ponds. Fill the hole with dirt after the chemical has seeped away. If pits were used for the treatment, punch holes in the plastic liners, and fill the pits with dirt after the solutions have seeped away.

Paste Preservatives

Forestry experiment tests show that poles set in the ground or concrete, for longest life should be pressure-treated, though they too benefit from the supplementary ground-line treatment described below.

Many who build pole buildings, however, find that pressure-treated poles are out of reach — by distance and/or

cost. Utility poles (that have been pressure-treated), discarded because of broken ends, may be long enough for building use if not too large in diameter. They too can be given supplementary preservative treatment.

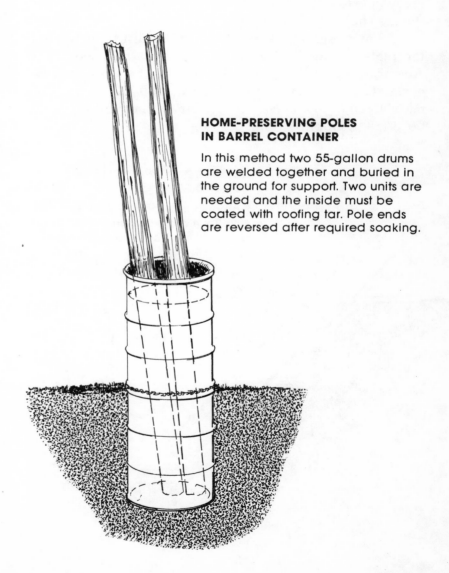

HOME-PRESERVING POLES IN BARREL CONTAINER

In this method two 55-gallon drums are welded together and buried in the ground for support. Two units are needed and the inside must be coated with roofing tar. Pole ends are reversed after required soaking.

The new paste preservatives can be applied effectively (to protect at the ground level) to green, dip-preserved and pressure-treated poles alike. Field tests show that several of these pastes will extend the three-year life of an untreated green pole to fifteen years. Used on previously treated poles, the life should be even more.

Paste preservatives are much the easiest to apply, and the materials to do nine poles will cost only about $24. Among the pastes showing the best test results are *Osmo-plastic* (Osmose Wood Preserving Co., 980 Ellicott St., Buffalo, N.Y. 14209) and *Pol-Nu* (Chapman Chemical Co., P.O. Box 9158, Memphis, Tenn. 38109).

The poles are set (see page 41) and are paste-treated before embedding. Thus older pole buildings — with some digging — can be re-treated periodically before deterioration begins.

Paste preservatives are very caustic, and one should wear protective clothing, goggles and a breathing filter.

The pole is well coated with the paste from eighteen inches below ground level to three to six inches above it. Then the coated area is wrapped with sheet plastic or plastic-backed kraft paper, which is stapled to the pole. Then the pole is embedded (see page 46).

Poles which have been treated as outlined on page 14 should be considered "permanent," except in their embedded sections. Paste applications to these areas about every ten years, however, should eliminate the worry of pole failures.

HOME-PRESERVING POLES IN GROUND PIT

Framework for pits is made of 1 x 4s with 2 x 4 blocks for strength. Pits are dug to fit the frameworks and are lined with heavy plastic sheeting.

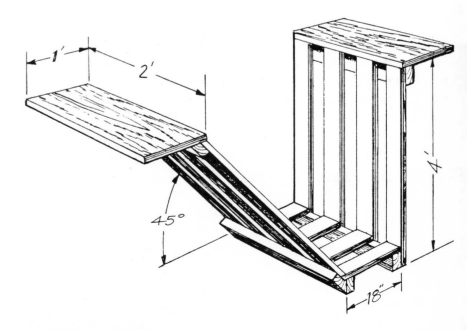

The Fastenings to Use

The fastening used in pole construction may be limited to nails and spikes, or include also bolts or lag screws or even patented special fasteners. The choice usually will depend upon costs and availability as well as the labor factors involved.

At framing areas where side stress might be expected, the use of bolts or lag screws should give rigidity superior to spikes or special fasteners.

Nails & Bolts: For all practical purposes there is no difference in the *shearing* strength of bolts, lag screws or spikes, providing the total diameters are about the same. For example, three 60d spikes, which have a diameter of $5/16$ inch, will equal the strength of a $3/4$-inch bolt, where the load on these fastenings is primarily vertical. As an assurance against spikes working loose, use cement-coated spikes or "barn spikes", which have a screw-like shank.

The choice of fasteners lies primarily in which is easier for you. Lead holes should be drilled for spikes, particularly near the ends of planks, to prevent splitting. This can be done on the ground, whereas holes for bolts that go through the poles must be drilled after the poles have been erected.

Following is a schedule of recommended sizes of nails for fastening various members together and for applying covering material. This data, listed in the U.S.D.A. Handbook No. 364, is the general standard of the building trades. The size of nails here are listed by penny number or "d", and whether common, finishing or galvanized, are the same equivalent lengths.

RECOMMENDED NAIL SIZES

| Joining | Nailing method | NAILS | | |
		Number	Size	Placement
Header to joist	End-nail	3	16d	
Joist to sill or girder	Toenail	2–3	10d or	
			8d	
Header and stringer joist to sill	Toenail		10d	16 inches on center.
Bridging to joist	Toenail each end	2	8d	
Ledger strip to beam, 2 inches thick		3	16d	At each joist.
Subfloor, boards:				
1 by 6 inches and smaller		2	8d	To each joist.
1 by 8 inches		3	8d	To each joist.
Subfloor, plywood:				
At edges			8d	6 inches on center.
At intermediate joists			8d	8 inches on center.
Subfloor (2 by 6 inches, T&G) to joist or girder	Blind-nail (casing) and face-nail.	2	16d	

RECOMMENDED NAIL SIZES

Joining	Nailing method	NAILS		Placement
		Number	Size	
Soleplate to stud, horizontal assembly	End-nail	2	16d	At each stud.
Top plate to stud	End-nail	2	16d	
Stud to soleplate	Toenail	4	8d	
Soleplate to joist or blocking	Face-nail		16d	16 inches on center.
Doubled studs	Face-nail, stagger		10d	16 inches on center.
End stud of intersecting wall to exterior wall stud	Face-nail		16d	16 inches on center.
Upper top plate to lower top plate	Face-nail		16d	16 inches on center.
Upper top plate, laps and intersections	Face-nail	2	16d	
Continuous header, 2 pieces, each edge			12d	12 inches on center.
Ceiling joist to top wall plates	Toenail	3	8d	
Ceiling joist laps at partition	Face-nail	4	16d	
Rafter to top plate	Toenail	2	8d	
Rafter to ceiling joist	Face-nail	5	10d	
Rafter to valley or hip rafter	Toenail	3	10d	
Ridge board to rafter	End-nail	3	10d	
Rafter to rafter through ridge board	Toenail	4	8d	
	Edge-nail	1	10d	
Collar beam to rafter:				
2-inch member	Face-nail	2	12d	
1-inch member	Face-nail	3	8d	
1-inch diagonal let-in brace to each stud and plate (4 nails at top).		2	8d	
Built-up corner studs:				
Studs to blocking	Face-nail	2	10d	Each side.
Intersecting stud to corner studs	Face-nail		16d	12 inches on center.
Built-up girders and beams, 3 or more members	Face-nail		20d	32 inches on center, each side.
Wall sheathing:				
1 by 8 inches or less, horizontal	Face-nail	2	8d	At each stud.
1 by 6 inches or greater, diagonal	Face-nail	3	8d	At each stud.
Wall sheathing, vertically applied plywood:				
⅜ inch and less thick	Face-nail		6d	6-inch edge.
½ inch and over thick	Face-nail		8d	12-inch intermediate.
Wall sheathing, vertically applied fiberboard:				
½ inch thick	Face-nail			1½-inch roofing nail.*
25/32 inch thick	Face-nail			1¾-inch roofing nail.*
Roof sheathing, boards, 4-, 6-, 8-inch width	Face-nail	2	8d	At each rafter.
Roof sheathing plywood:				
⅜ inch and less thick	Face-nail		6d	6-inch edge and 12-
½ inch and over thick	Face-nail		8d	inch intermediate.

*3 inch edge and 6 inch intermediate.

Metal Fastenings

Illustrated on these two pages is a variety of manufactured metal devices, these developed by Teco (5530 Wisconsin Ave., Washington, D.C. 20015). Such fasteners often simplify construction, save time, and in some cases save on materials. For instance, by using joist hangers rather than nailing the joists to the top of the plates, the total height of the wall will be reduced by the width of the plate. Other devices can provide supplementary or additional strength in joining rafters to plates or in tying across the ridge pole.

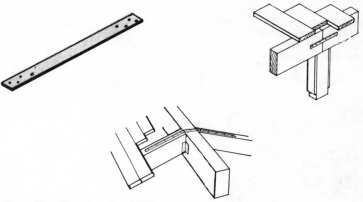

Strap Tie   This simple metal strap is perhaps the most versatile fastener and may be used for connecting many types of framing joints.

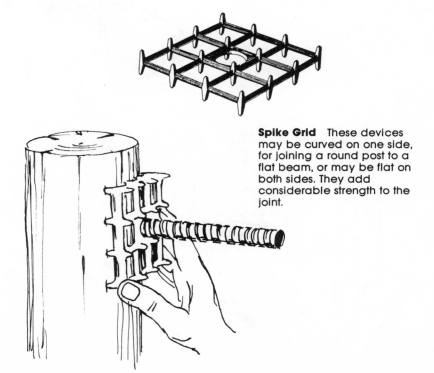

Spike Grid   These devices may be curved on one side, for joining a round post to a flat beam, or may be flat on both sides. They add considerable strength to the joint.

Flat plate connector   This device is especially useful for splicing beams together or for joining a flat beam to a round post in a top load situation.

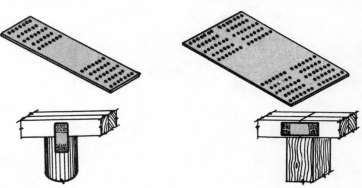

Rafter Anchor These are used to anchor the building's rafters to the wall studs and also have application as tie-down devices.

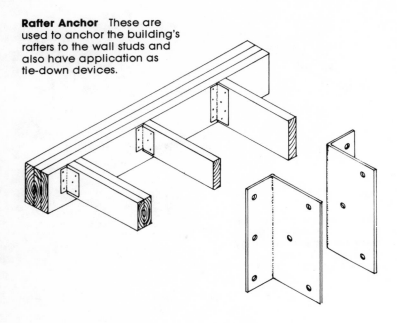

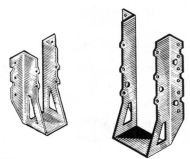

Joist and Beam Anchor This is a specialized anchor which is available in sizes to fit most dimensions of lumber.

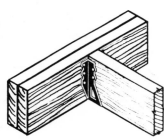

Angles These fasteners come in many variations and are very handy for joining rafters to beams and also for attaching plates and rafters to the ridge.

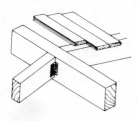

Anchor This is a variation of the All-Purpose Framing anchor, and might be used in attaching floor joists (as shown) to sills.

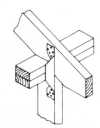

Triple Grip Framing Anchor This device is used in the same applications as the All-Purpose Framing Anchor, but it provides one additional nailing surface.

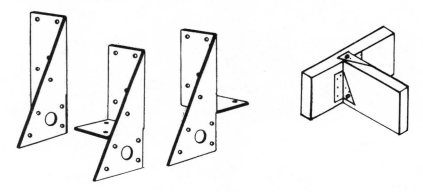

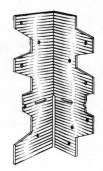

All-Purpose Framing Anchor This fastener, like the Strap Tie, may be used in a number of applications, such as attaching joists to plates and roof trusses to plates.

Plywood Supports These fasteners are especially time-saving for leveling plywood. Their use eliminates the need for blocking at the joints.

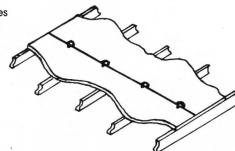

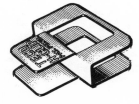

Framing Anchor These fasteners are used primarily for tying rafters to plates, but can be used to anchor many other types of connections.

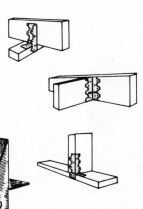

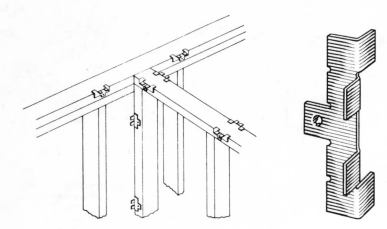

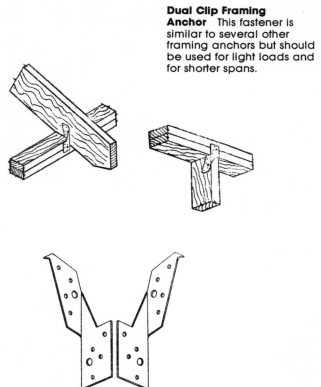

Dual Clip Framing Anchor   This fastener is similar to several other framing anchors but should be used for light loads and for shorter spans.

Backup Clip   In a similar way to the Supports this device provides a support for dry wall construction or paneling at the wall corners and ceiling joints.

PART TWO

Pole Homes On Camera

TWO VACATION HOUSES

Homes based upon the pole construction principle are going up in all sections of the United States today, in large part because of the economy, the high suitability to sloping terrain and the flexibility of design that the pole method allows.

The two unusual pole houses shown here are located thousands of miles apart—in Massachusetts and in Hawaii. The photographic record is provided by the Koppers Company, which makes the chemicals employed in the pressure treatment of the poles and other structural woods that went into these handsome homes. Plans to construct these two homes are not included here because of the buildings' specialized designs and applications.

The Hawaiian home of Gordon R. Steen, reminiscent of native Polynesian house design, provides for efficient natural ventilation through ceiling ducts. The pressure-treated poles (here using a water-borne salt preservative) are unpainted and reach from their footings on the steep slope to the high roof beams.

Construction from start to finish took about eight weeks. The outside and interior poles were set first, roof beams were then attached, the deck system cantilevered from the poles, floors bolted to the poles and the walls attached last.

Architects for the home were Black, Pagliuso, Kikuchi and O'Dowd of Honolulu.

This vacation home for a family of five overlooks Hingham Bay near Boston. The extremely narrow and steeply sloping lot led Architect Richard Owen Abbott to employ pole construction and a highly unusual interior design.

The Hull house is 81 feet long but only 12 feet wide. A deck runs along the waterfront side, which itself is 75 per cent glass. The back of the house is shingled but without windows. Louvers provide ventilation.

The back of the home rests on a cement pier bearing wall, while the front is supported by eleven 30-foot poles which have been pressure-treated with Koppers' pentachlorophenal in liquified butane.

End view of Massachusetts home shows the steepness of the lot
and the narrow dimension of the home.

Interior of the long, narrow house is divided into eight bays of about 10 by 12 feet each. Only the bathroom is partitioned. Walkway along the waterfront side expands into a deck, right foreground.

Triangular deck at house's center is seen from the steep slope below.
Note that the treated poles are set in concrete.

MASSACHUSETTS HOME

Central living area
overlooks the deck to the
harbor and a nature
reserve in left distance.
Note plates supporting
roof rafters are bolted to
both sides of the wall
poles.

HAWAIIAN HOME

Each room of the elevated
Hawaiian home opens
on a deck. Access to
the house is by stairway
from above.

HAWAIIAN HOME EXTERIOR

Long poles support the
floor joists, the extensive
decking, the roof rafters
and the walls. The wide
eaves protect windows
and deck areas from
direct sun and rain.

HAWAIIAN INTERIOR

The airy, open inside roof area also allows updraft ventilation. Note that the heavy beams are attached with structural metal anchors to each other and to the interior support poles.

HAWAIIAN BEDROOM

Tropical forest lies just outside this corner bedroom's deck. The textured redwood walls hang from inside faces of exterior poles, as does the decking.

PART THREE

How to
Do it

Getting Started

While detailed plans for certain kinds of pole buildings appear later in Part IV, this may be a good time to run through the steps of pole construction in general. This will give an overview that will help explain what pole construction entails, and what to look for in plans.

This description assumes the building to be on fairly level ground, but with a slight slope for good drainage. It is wise in constructing any building (pole or conventional) to avoid low-lying ground with a high water table. Also avoid heavy, wet clay soil if you can. Sandy gravel is best, as is shown in the Tables on pages 38 and 40. Hillside pole construction requires different pole embedment techniques, which are pictured later and are noted by the Table on page 39.

Layout for the Poles

To begin with, of course, all of the tools that will be used, as well as all materials needed for the completed framing and roofing, should be assembled on the site. If you are going to bolt the plates to poles (see Page 44) or pre-bore nail holes (Page 44), a temporary electric power source will be helpful. This is to allow the use of an electric drill and later, in the sheathing work, an electric saw. If the building will not have electric service, of course both functions can be accomplished with hand tools. Hand-boring at elevation for the ridge plates, is difficult, however, when working from a ladder rather than scaffolding. See suggested tool list on page 100.

You start to lay out the building by setting up batter boards at the far corners. Run strings between the batter boards to outline the building, as shown on page 35.

Square the corners with care by means of a builder's triangle (see illustration) and, to use lumber efficiently, with sides of 6, 8 and 10 feet, or any multiples of 3, 4 and 5 feet. These string guidelines serve to locate the holes for the outer poles.

Each of the building plans which follows shows in the Floor Plans the distances between the poles. Often there are extra, close-set poles to frame doorways, but in general—if you are making your own plans—pole distances and plate sizes should be determined by applying the Maximum Span Chart on Page 56. Long spans may present problems of sidewall rigidity, but this can be compensated for by using extra girts (see page 51).

Long pole spans will impose added loads from the roof rafters to the eaves plates. Therefore, as pole distances are increased, it is advisable to increase the dimensions of the eaves plate stock (such as from 2 x 8s to 2 x 10s, or 2 x 10s to 2 x 12s) as shown in the Page 56 Chart. The same is true for sill plates if heavy floor loads are anticipated.

If the plans and dimensions given in this book are modified, or if you are developing your own new plans, try to keep distances to match standard lumber lengths in order to minimize waste. Board and timber ends are useful, however, for blocking, shims, etc.

It should be noted here that in working with any pole plans it is difficult to control the building's precise dimen-

LAYOUT FOR THE POLES WITH BATTER BOARDS

You start the layout of a pole building by the use of batter boards at the corners, just as in the construction of a conventional building.

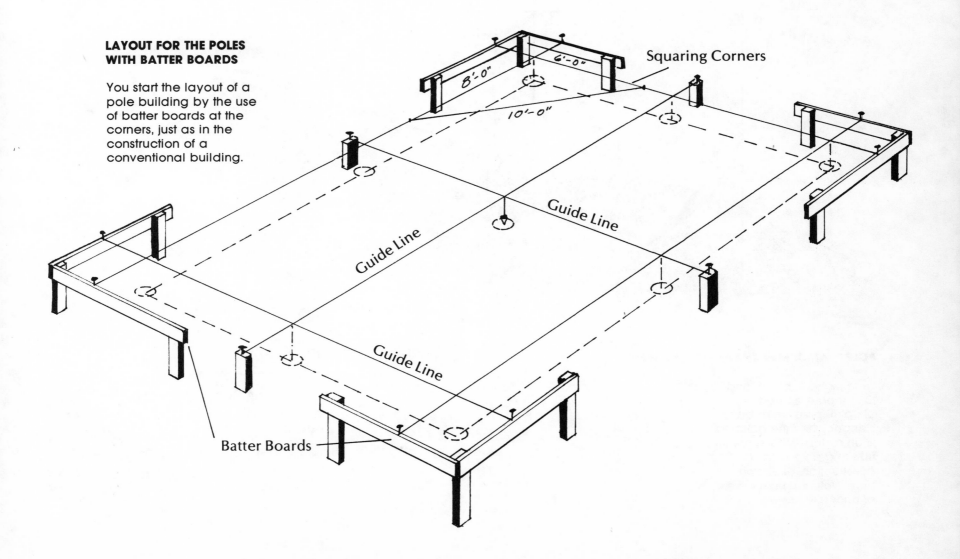

Squaring Corners

8'-0"

6'-0"

10'-0"

Guide Line

Guide Line

Guide Line

Batter Boards

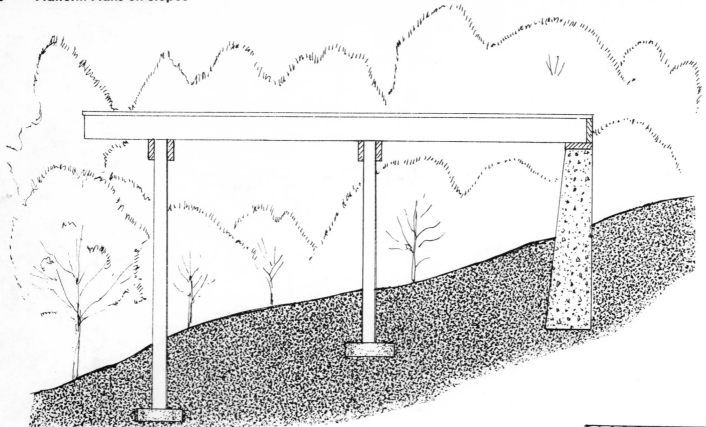

POLE PLATFORM PLAN ON STEEP SLOPE

Note in the Tables B and C that pole embedment of uphill poles must be deeper when the building is on a slope. The same is true in a pole platform construction, as shown here. Note the uphill use of concrete keywall.

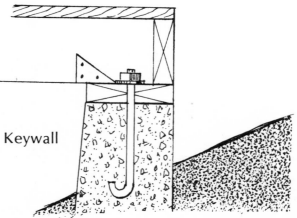

Keywall

sions on the basis of distances from center to center of the poles. This is because the poles may vary by an inch or two in diameter at a given height. Therefore, if it is important to hold a building to exact dimensions, measure distances from the outside to outside of the poles, and add side shims to bring widths up to the set dimensions.

Determine the location of the poles from the plans, and measure the spacing of poles on the guidelines.

Drop a plumb bob from the measured spacing and, for the outside poles, mark the center of the pole holes 5 or 6 inches in from these points by means of small stakes.

When all the pole hole positions are marked by stakes, remove all the interior guidelines. Now you are ready to dig your holes and set the poles. The width of your building will determine whether or not the plans call for interior poles, as well as the type of rafters or trusses needed.

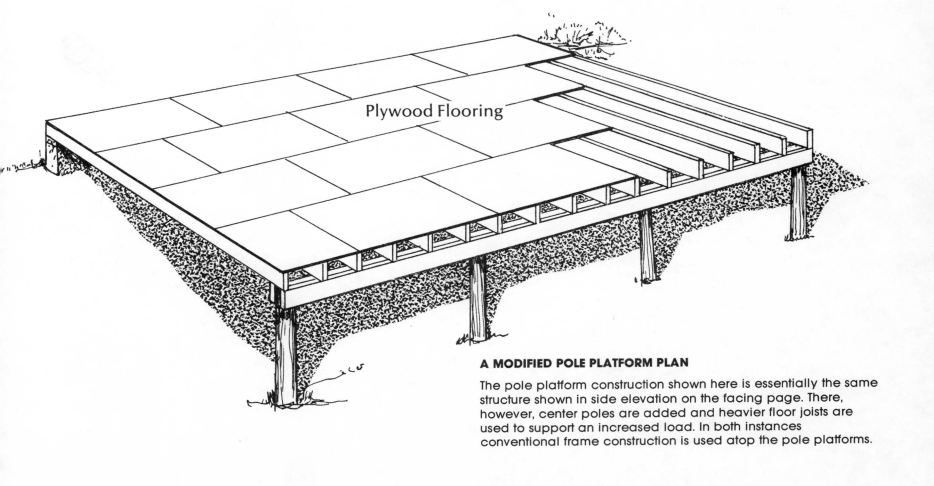

Plywood Flooring

A MODIFIED POLE PLATFORM PLAN

The pole platform construction shown here is essentially the same structure shown in side elevation on the facing page. There, however, center poles are added and heavier floor joists are used to support an increased load. In both instances conventional frame construction is used atop the pole platforms.

Planning and Digging the Holes

The first thing to consider even before starting to dig, is the general soil condition of the site; secondly its grade.

In general for any pole building, the soil is considered below average if it is soft clay, poorly compacted sand, or clay containing large amounts of silt (with water standing during a wet period). Average soil is compact, well-graded sand and gravel, hard clay or graded fine and coarse sand.

Pole buildings based on the criteria in Table A are suitable on sites that are flat or with a grade of less than 1 in 10. In all the Tables:

H= Unsupported height of poles (from ground to first cross member).

A = Embedment depth, using backfill or tamped earth, sand, gravel or crushed rock.

B = Embedment depth, using backfill of concrete or soil cement.

D = Bearing Diameter (size of pad).

Pole buildings based on the criteria shown in Tables B and C can be built on sites with slopes as steep as 1 in 1, provided there is no danger from landslides.

Table B shows the embedment depths for the longer, downhill poles, which carry only vertical loads.

Table C shows the criteria for the uphill line of poles in a steep site, that must be embedded adequately to resist lateral as well as vertical loads.

TABLE A
DEPTH OF EMBEDMENT

"H"	Pole Spacing	GOOD SOIL				AVERAGE SOIL				BELOW AVERAGE SOIL			
		Embedment Depth		"D"	Tip Size	Embedment Depth		"D"	Tip Size	Embedment Depth		"D"	Tip Size
		A	B			A	B			A	B		
1-½'	8'	5.0'	4.0'	18''	6.5''	6.0'	5.0'	24''	6''	—	6.0'	36''	6''
to	10'	5.5'	4.0'	21''	7''	7.0'	5.0'	30''	7''	—	6.5'	42''	7''
3'	12'	6.0'	4.5'	24''	7''	7.5'	5.5'	36''	7''	—	7.0'	48''	7''
3'	8'	6.0'	4.0'	18''	7''	7.5'	5.5'	24''	7''	—	7.0'	36''	7''
to	10'	6.0'	4.5'	21''	8''	8.0'	6.0'	30''	8''	—	7.5'	42''	8''
8'	12'	6.5'	5.0'	24''	8''	—	6.0'	36''	8''	—	8.0'	48''	8''

— Embedment depth required is greater than 8 feet, and considered excessively expensive.

TABLE B
SLOPE EMBEDMENT

	SLOPE OF GRADE		
Soil Strength	Up to 1:3	Up to 1:2	Up to 1:1
Below Average	4.5'	6.0'	—
Average	4.0'	5.0'	7.0'
Good	4.0'	4.0'	6.0'

TABLE C
SPACING & DEPTH RELATIONS

"H"	Pole Spacing	GOOD SOIL				AVERAGE SOIL				BELOW AVERAGE SOIL			
		Embedment Depth A	B	"D"	Tip Size	Embedment Depth A	B	"D"	Tip Size	Embedment Depth A	B	"D"	Tip Size
1-½' to 3'	6'	7.0'	5.0'	18"	8"	—	6.5'	18"	8"	—	—	—	—
	8'	7.5'	5.5'	18"	9"	—	7.0'	24"	9"	—	—	—	—
	10'	—	6.0'	21"	9"	—	8.0'	30"	9"	—	—	—	—
	12'	—	6.5'	24"	10"*	—	—	—	—	—	—	—	—
3' to 8'	6'	7.5'	5.5'	18"	8"	—	7.0'	18"	8"	—	—	—	—
	8'	8.0'	6.0'	18"	9"	—	8.0'	24"	9"	—	—	—	—
	10'	—	7.0'	21"	10"*	—	—	—	—	—	—	—	—
	12'	—	7.0'	24"	11"*	—	—	—	—	—	—	—	—

— Embedment depth required is greater than 8 feet, and considered excessively expensive.
* These tip diameters may be decreased by one inch providing embedment is increased by one-half foot.

TABLE D
EMBEDMENT FOR FRAME BUILDING

"H"	Pole Spacing	GOOD SOIL				AVERAGE SOIL				BELOW AVERAGE SOIL			
		Embedment Depth		"D"	Tip Size	Embedment Depth		"D"	Tip Size	Embedment Depth		"D"	Tip Size
		A	B			A	B			A	B		
1-½'	8'	4.0'	4.0'	18"	5"	5.5'	4.0'	24"	5"	7.0'	5.0'	36"	5"
to	10'	4.5'	4.0'	21"	5"	6.0'	4.0'	30"	5"	8.0'	5.5'	42"	5"
3'	12'	5.0'	4.0'	24"	5"	6.5'	4.5'	36"	5"	—	5.5'	48"	5"
3'	8'	5.0'	4.0'	18"	6"	6.5'	4.5'	24"	6"	—	6.0'	36"	6"
to	10'	5.5'	4.0'	21"	7"	7.0'	5.0'	30"	7"	—	6.5'	42"	7"
8'	12'	6.0'	4.5'	24"	7"	7.5'	5.5'	36"	7"	—	7.0'	48"	7"

— Embedment depth required is greater than 8 feet, and considered excessively expensive.

Pole platforms (those on which conventional frame buildings rest) are based on the criteria shown in Table D. They are suitable on sites with a flat grade, or less than a 1 in 10 slope.

Selecting the Poles

Pole holes may be dug by hand or by one of several mechanical means. Hand digging or very careful machine digging protects tree roots, top soil and the soil structure around the poles.

Poles taper, and you will set the larger or butt ends in the ground. Dig holes 6 to 8 inches larger in diameter than the butt of the pole. If the holes are of any considerable depth, however, they will have to be wider than that to allow digging room, unless a power auger or pole shovels are used, and also to allow for a punch pad (see Tables pages 38, 39 and 40).

A rule of thumb is that the depth of the pole in the ground should be 4 feet when the eaves of the building will not be over 10 feet from the ground. When the eaves will be more than 10 feet, the poles should be embedded to a depth of 5 feet. However, the most important guide to the depth of the poles is the frost line in your locality. In Vermont, for instance, poles for any building should be embedded at least 4 feet, regardless of where the eaves are. Also, as shown in Tables B and C (page 39), poles for hillside buildings require deeper embedment than those for a level site.

In selecting your poles you will find those of 5 or 6 inches in diameter at the top are adequate for most buildings. For any pole up to 16 feet in length, a 4 or 5-inch top diameter will be sufficient. The pole always should be 2 or 3 feet longer than the distance from the bottom of the hole to the roof. The top later will be cut off flush with the rafters.

Setting and Aligning the Poles

Your plan or the soil condition may require that in each pole hole you have a concrete pad at the bottom. A good rule here is to pour the pad half as thick as the diameter of the hole. Its diameter may be determined from the Tables on pages 38, 39 and 40.

Do not set the poles until the concrete has cured.

Pick out the straightest poles for the corners of the building. Then with block and tackle (and/or a few strong friends) insert the outside poles first. Then insert the inside poles if they are required.

Rotate each pole so that the straightest side faces out. Use a wrapped rope and wood lever bar. A peavey may tear the wood. Shovel a small amount of soil around the pole and tamp lightly—just enough to keep the butt end from shifting. Complete embedment of the poles is *not* done at this time.

Align the poles vertically with a carpenter's level placed on a straight-edge held against the outer face. Nail temporary braces to the poles and to stakes in the ground, to keep the poles lined up until framing is completed. Locate this bracing in areas where it won't interfere with the work.

PUNCH PADS FOR THE POLES

Heavy flat stone or poured cement punch pad should be provided for each of the pole holes before the poles are placed.

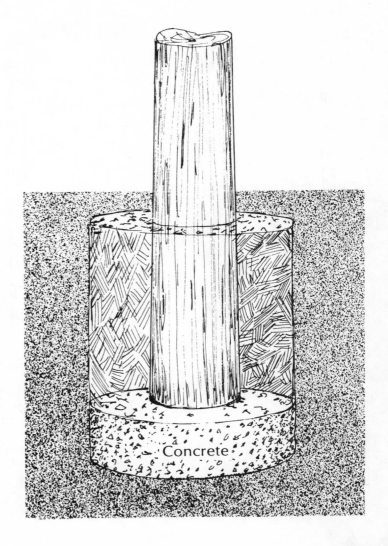

Concrete

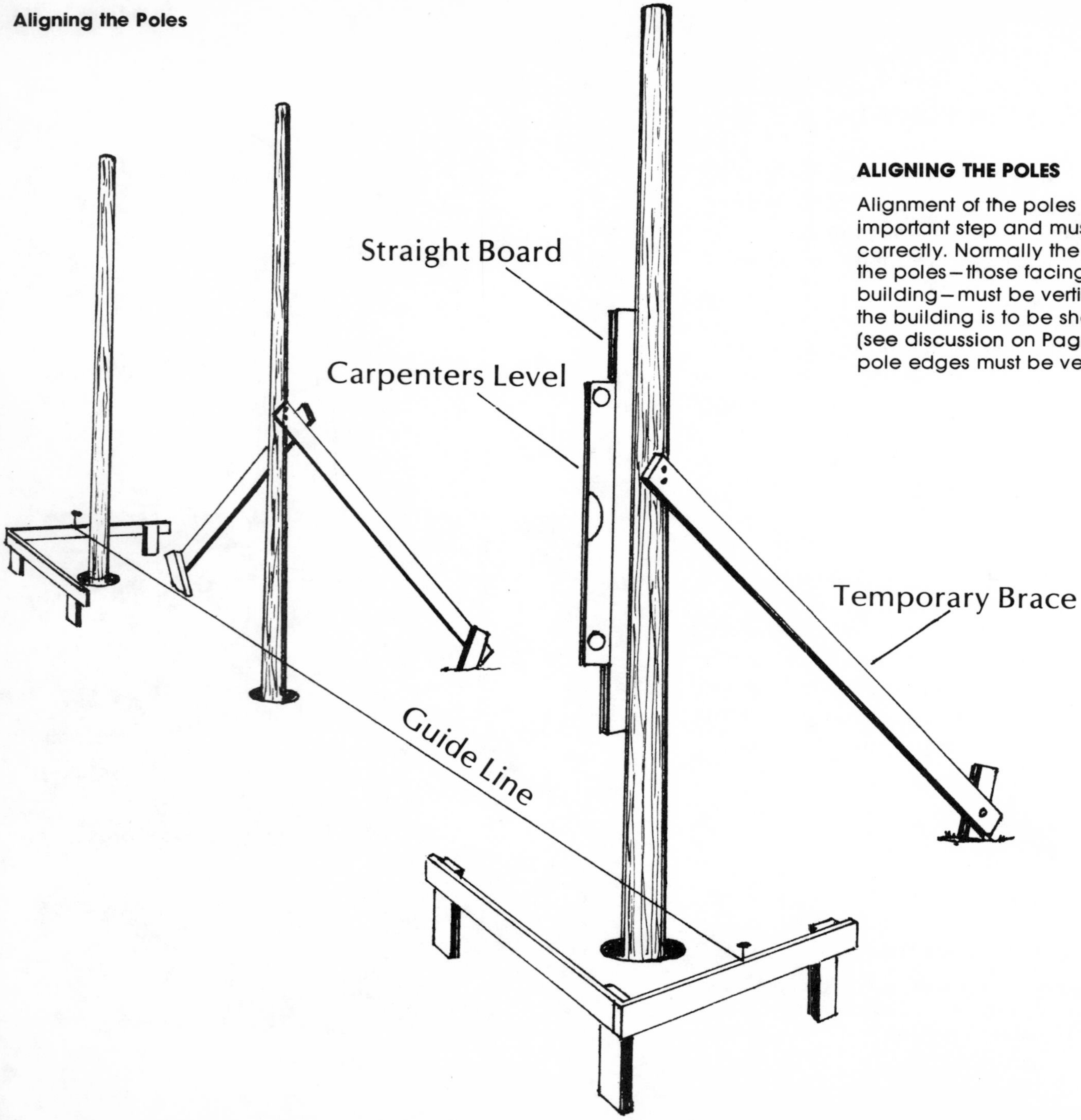

Straight Board

Carpenters Level

Temporary Brace

Guide Line

ALIGNING THE POLES

Alignment of the poles is a very important step and must be done correctly. Normally the outside edge of the poles—those facing away from the building—must be vertical. However, if the building is to be sheathed inside (see discussion on Page 90), the inside pole edges must be vertical.

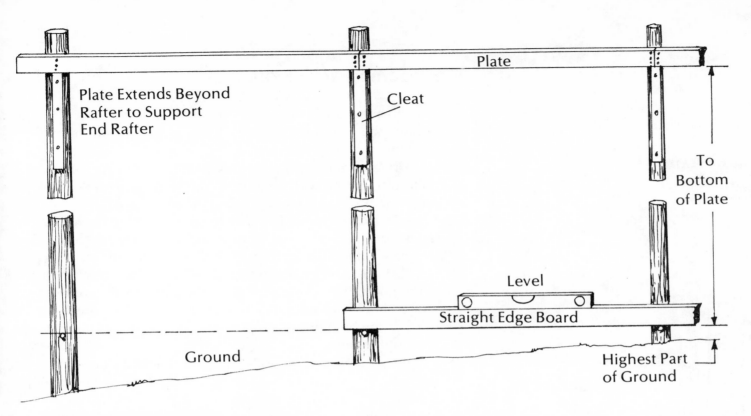

Plate

Plate Extends Beyond
Rafter to Support
End Rafter

Cleat

To
Bottom
of Plate

Level

Straight Edge Board

Ground

Highest Part
of Ground

GETTING THE GROUND LEVEL

Carpenter's Level establishes true line for sill.

ANOTHER LEVELING METHOD

Sliding level on string establishes true line.

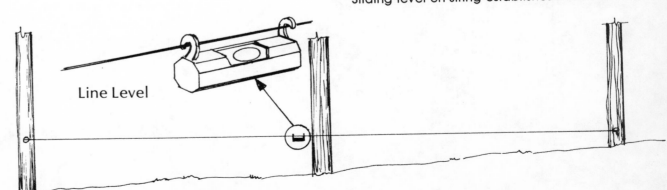

Line Level

Attaching Wall Plates

The outside plates at the eaves should be attached first. Determine the height for these plates by measuring up from a level line this way:

Drive a nail in a pole a few inches above the highest point of ground. With a straight-edge and carpenter's level establish this level point on all the poles in the wall. Nail a 2 x 4 or a 2 x 6 cleat (about 36 inches long) with its top flush with the measured height from your ground line to the bottom of the plate's intended location. This cleat is temporary.

Plates should be cut so that their ends will butt together at the poles, with the exception of the plates at the corners. These should be extended beyond the poles on the long sides of the building to support the end rafters on the outsides of the poles.

Rest the plates on the cleats and nail or bolt them to the poles. Now remove the temporary cleats. Pre-boring the nail holes in the plates will minimize the danger of splitting the wood, yet will not decrease the holding power. Use a $^5/_{32}$-inch drill for 40 d nails. Plates on the *inside* of the wall poles are not attached until the rafters are in place.

When heavy snow weight or exceptional winds may be expected, or where load-bearing floors are supported by the poles, bolts are advised instead of nailing to attach plates and floor sills to the poles (see data on page 17). Lag screws with washers may be so used, also.

Ridge Plates

Follow the same general procedure for the ridge plates as you did for the wall plates. Determine the height of the

SETTING FLOOR JOISTS ON PLATES

More details on this Step are given under Floor Construction.

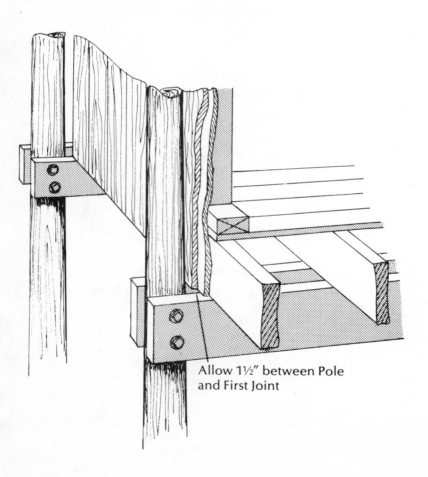

Allow 1½" between Pole and First Joint

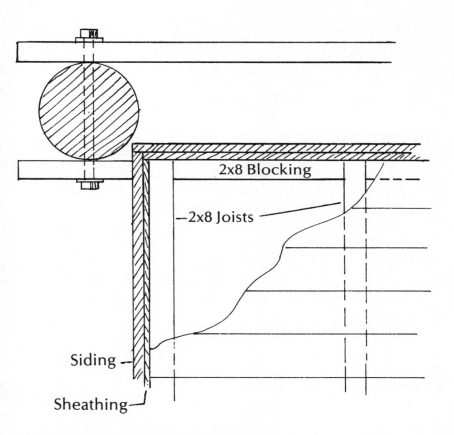

2x8 Blocking

—2x8 Joists

Siding

Sheathing

ATTACHING SILL PLATES TO POLES

Walls go inside the poles when finished
walls inside are needed.

bottom of the ridge plates (as for the wall plates), and nail
cleats of 2x4 lumber on each side of the center pole. Rest the
plates on the cleats and proceed to fasten them as with the
wall plates with spikes, bolts or lag screws.

Inner Pole Plates

When the building is so wide as to require extra inner poles,
the position of the plates on these intermediate poles should

LOCATING PLATE ON INTERIOR POLES

If the building has center
poles, locate ridge plates
first on the outside poles.
Then a taut string run
between them, as shown,
will easily establish the
location for the ridge
plates on the center
poles.

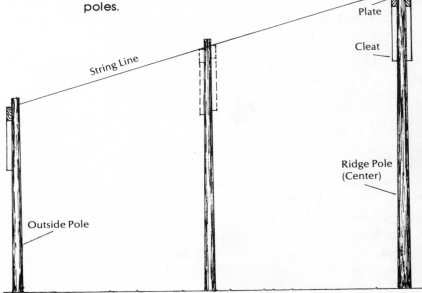

Plate

Cleat

String Line

Ridge Pole
(Center)

Outside Pole

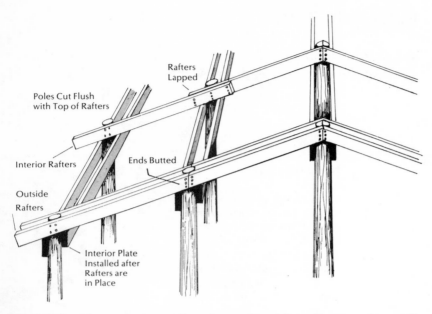

Poles Cut Flush with Top of Rafters

Rafters Lapped

Interior Rafters

Ends Butted

Outside Rafters

Interior Plate Installed after Rafters are in Place

be located by running a line from the ridge plate to the wall plate. Attach cleats and plates on both sides to correspond with this line.

Rafters

Rafters are placed on the outside of the end wall poles and should be butted to provide a smooth base for exterior siding. Extend the lower rafters over the outside plates at the eaves to provide an overhang—usually about 10 to 14 inches. Cut the butt ends of the outside rafters to the proper angle so that the rafters may be nailed to the poles. Intermediate rafters may be lapped. Rafters adjacent to a pole should be nailed to the pole.

When rafters are in place, the poles should be cut off flush with the tops of the rafters. Anchor other rafters to the plates by means of metal straps or by 2-inch scab boards (or ties), fitted between the rafters.

Pole Embedment

Proper setting and embedment of the poles is crucial to the strength of the building's frame. After the rafters are in place, now complete the pole embedment.

You may backfill around the poles with the soil dug from the holes, or the backfilling may be done with concrete, soil cement, pea gravel or crushed rock. Clean sand is least expensive and achieves 100 per cent compaction when flooded with water, providing the surrounding soil offers good drainage.

When earth is used it must be compacted, a little at a time, by wetting and careful tamping. Over-embedding, however, or use of much concrete, defeats the inherent economy of the pole system.

Backfilling with soil cement is an economical way of achieving strength nearly equal to concrete. It is made by using earth free of organic matter and sifted to remove all pieces over one inch in size. Mix five parts of earth with one of cement. Then wet and mix it to a thick slurry and tamp it well into place around the poles.

Another method of embedment uses a "necklace" of concrete around the pole below the frost line. It can be cast after the poles are set but not fully filled in. This necklace should be at least 12 inches thick. A minimum of four one-inch diameter lag screws around the pole are required to transfer the vertical force to the necklace.

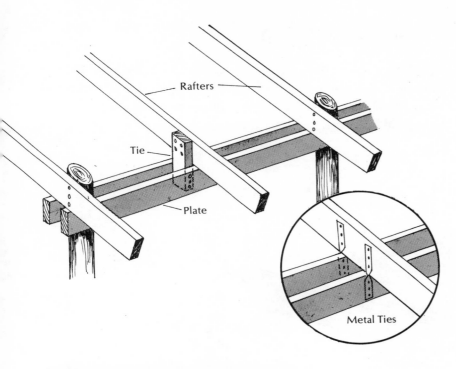

Rafters

Tie

Plate

Metal Ties

ATTACHING RAFTERS TO POLE PLATES

Attachment of rafters
above the pole plates is
shown here, and in detail
the rafter overhang at
eaves.

The necklace method is practical only in areas where the frost line does not exceed 2 feet. It would be exceedingly difficult to cast such a necklace at a depth of three feet or more.

When embedment of the poles has been completed the temporary pole braces are removed.

USING A POLE NECKLACE

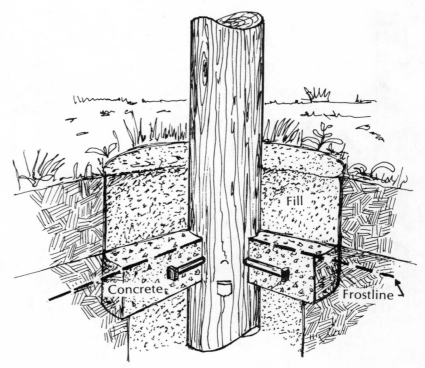

Fill

Concrete

Frostline

Inside Wall Plates

After the lower rafters are in place, the inside plates on the eaves should be installed. Push the plates up against the rafters and nail or bolt them to the poles, as shown in the illustration for rafters on page 46.

Permanent Bracing

Knee braces or plywood gussets should be installed on the inside of the poles. Nail or bolt two pieces of 2 x 4 four feet long at each end, as illustrated. When there is a wide center space in the structure an additional knee brace or gusset

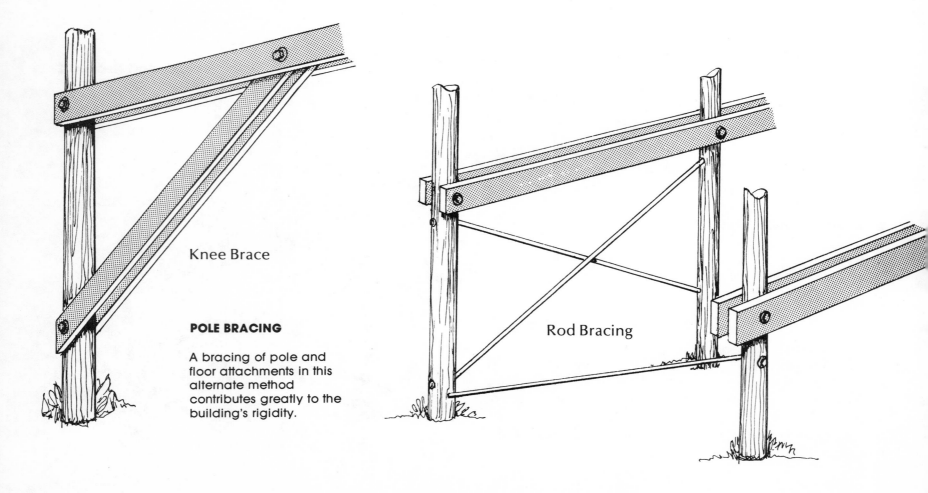

Knee Brace

POLE BRACING

A bracing of pole and floor attachments in this alternate method contributes greatly to the building's rigidity.

Rod Bracing

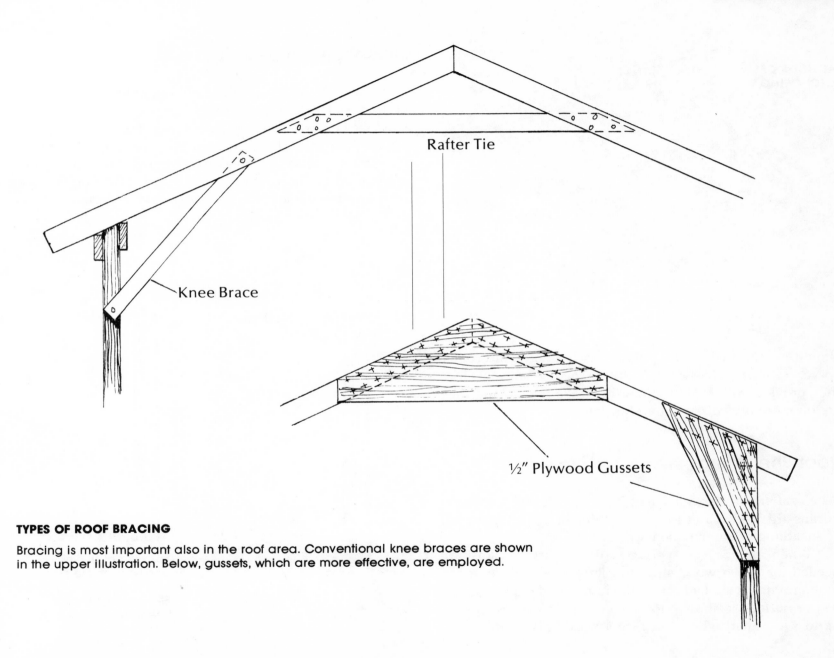

Rafter Tie

Knee Brace

½″ Plywood Gussets

TYPES OF ROOF BRACING

Bracing is most important also in the roof area. Conventional knee braces are shown in the upper illustration. Below, gussets, which are more effective, are employed.

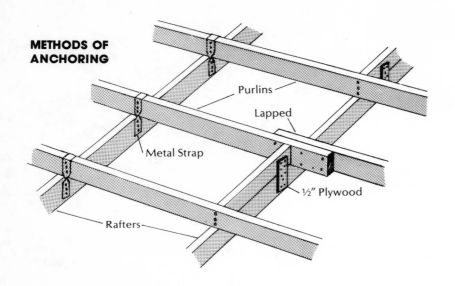

METHODS OF ANCHORING

Purlins

Lapped

Metal Strap

½" Plywood

Rafters

should be attached to the pole on each side of the center space, as shown. Gussets are better than knee bracing, since they provide greater strength at the hinge points, and they are no more difficult to cut and install.

Roof Sheathing

When rafters are spaced 2 feet on center (2 feet apart), no purlins are needed and 1-inch sheathing or ½-inch plywood of sheathing grade may be used.

When rafters are spaced further apart, purlins are needed for 1-inch wood sheathing, metal or other types of roofing. Purlins are laid across the rafters and either are lapped or butted, as shown. Rafters or purlins may be spaced up to 8 feet apart when 2-inch roof decking is used.

Side Wall Construction

If you want to have your pole building fully enclosed to the ground, start at the ground with splash boards. This is true whether you are planning an enclosed farm building, or to put skirting around the poles on which a house is built.

Starting about 3 inches under the ground line and extending up the wall, spike splash boards to the poles, using pressure-treated lumber or wood that is inherently rot-

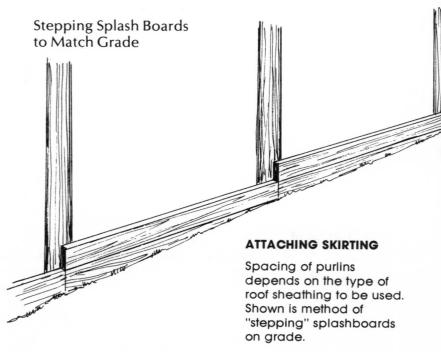

Stepping Splash Boards to Match Grade

ATTACHING SKIRTING

Spacing of purlins depends on the type of roof sheathing to be used. Shown is method of "stepping" splashboards on grade.

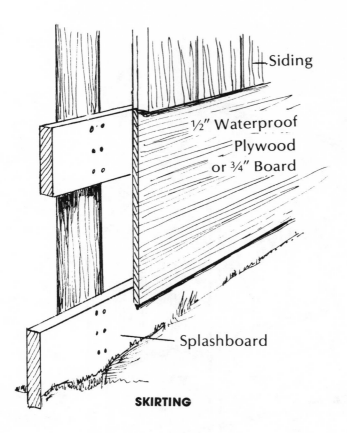

-Siding

½" Waterproof
Plywood
or ¾" Board

Splashboard

SKIRTING

DETAIL OF SPLASHBOARDS

Detail of splashboards and of exterior sheathing method is shown here. Note pressure-treated lumber should be placed below the ground line. In areas where there are termites use asbestos cement board buried in the earth.

ATTACHING GIRTS

Illustrated here is the use of girts between the poles to support the sidewall sheathing. Shown in cross-section is the reinforcement of a girt.

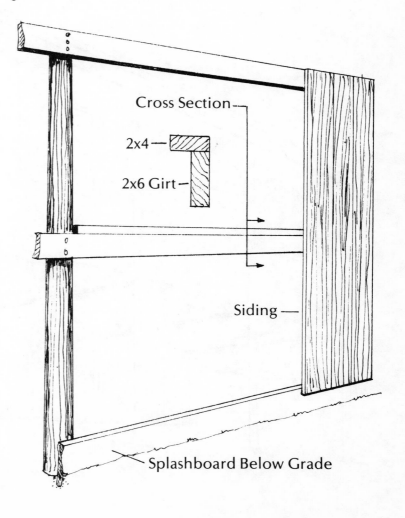

Cross Section-

2x4 -

2x6 Girt-

Siding -

Splashboard Below Grade

SUPPORTING UTILITY ROOM

Year-round Homes (see Plans on Pages 82 through 97) as well as Vacation Homes adapted to use in cold periods, can employ a utility room base. Further details on such construction are given on Page 74.

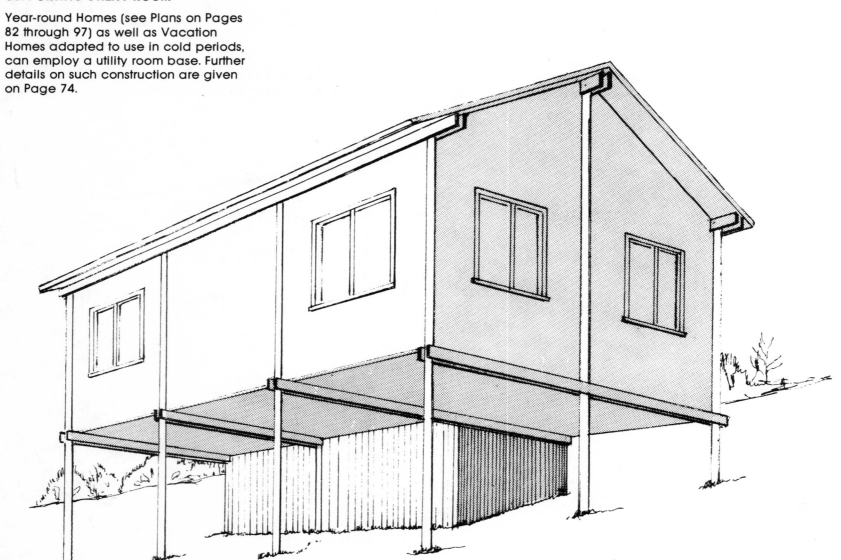

resistant (see page 12). These should be one or two 2 x 10 or 2 x 12 planks.

Girts for the siding are nailed across the poles above the splash boards. They should be spaced on 2 feet or 4 feet, depending upon the type of siding to be used. Generally speaking, metal siding will require 2-foot centers, while wood can be on 4-foot centers.

If the space between poles exceeds 6 feet, a 2 x 4 is placed (as illustrated) on each 2 x 6 for reinforcement. However, metal siding always will require more reinforcing than wood.

Vertical boards and battens (or other kinds of siding such as plywood or metal) then are attached to the girts. In any case, the top two inches of the splash boards should be overlapped by the side walls.

Reinforced girts usually provide adequate sidewall rigidity when spaced as close as two feet apart. Placement of vertical studs, toe-nailed to sill and eaves plates, will be used where windows interrupt the girts. Windows and exterior doors should be framed in with wall studs in any event.

Studs perform no weight-support role for either roof or floor, however, in pole construction. Safe pole distances and adequately heavy eaves and floor plates do it all.

Floor Construction and Insulation

Most pole buildings, unless a dirt floor is in order, will have a slab floor (see bottom illustration on Page 54) or a suspended floor, and if these buildings are to be located and used in cold climate areas, construction should be planned with the view to effective floor insulation. Methods of suspended floor joist attachment are shown on Page 53, while

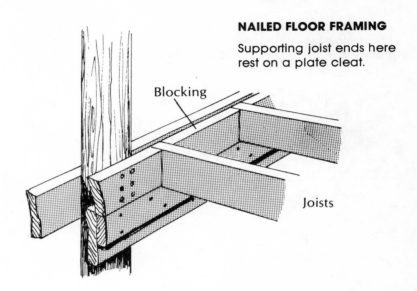

NAILED FLOOR FRAMING

Supporting joist ends here rest on a plate cleat.

Blocking

Joists

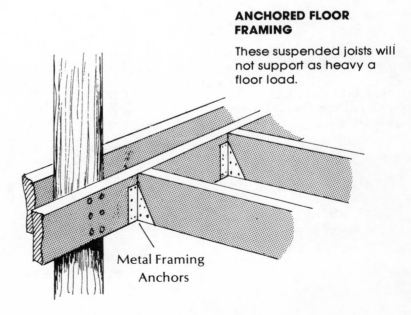

ANCHORED FLOOR FRAMING

These suspended joists will not support as heavy a floor load.

Metal Framing Anchors

FLOOR INSULATION

Open floor is insulated
from below with batts hung
between joists.

Alternate method places
rigid foam atop joists and
below flooring.

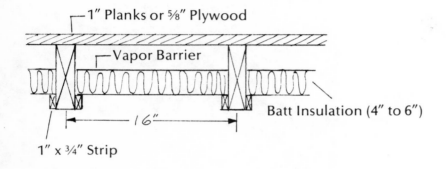

1″ Planks or ⅝″ Plywood

Vapor Barrier

1″ x ¾″ Strip

16″

Batt Insulation (4″ to 6″)

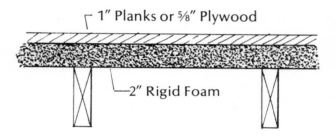

1″ Planks or ⅝″ Plywood

2″ Rigid Foam

Floor built on grade
requires vapor seal below
concrete.

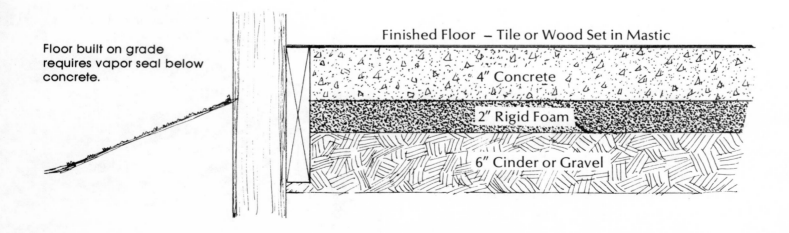

Finished Floor — Tile or Wood Set in Mastic

4″ Concrete

2″ Rigid Foam

6″ Cinder or Gravel

those which are illustrated on Page 44 will provide for greater floor loading. The chart on Page 56 provides safe formulae of load and support for both floors and roofs. In cold country take into account the weight of possible snow accumulations, particularly if the roof pitch is shallow.

In slab floor construction do not overlook the need to lay a vapor barrier of polyethylene sheeting under the slab. Otherwise the slab will absorb ground moisture, and some serious problems may develop later.

In climates where termites occur, ring cups may be placed around the poles and the wall skirting is not run down to the ground level.

Framing for Floors

Floors carrying heavy leads (see chart Page 56) will be stronger if supported by bolt or lag screw attachment, as shown on Page 44. The butting of joists to the sill plates, attached with metal strapping, as shown, would not be used except where light floor loads are planned. The overlapped joists rest on and are supported by the sill plates, and will have a greater load capacity.

Floor insulation

Methods of insulating suspended floors and those of slab construction are indicated here. See details on the latter also on Page 53. Note at left the use of dead air space to supplement the insulation.

INSULATING THE ROOF

Batt insulation is set between roof purlins, below sheathing.

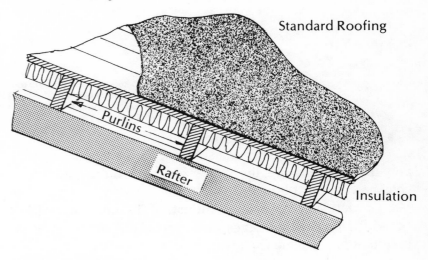

Standard Roofing

Purlins

Rafter

Insulation

Alternate method dispenses with batts, uses insulating plank in place of standard roof sheathing.

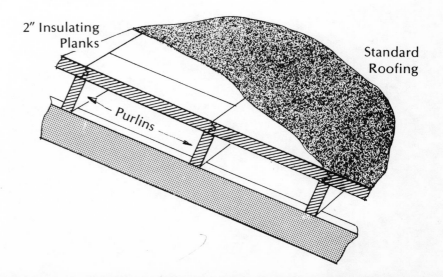

2" Insulating Planks

Standard Roofing

Purlins

MAXIMUM SPAN FLOOR JOISTS & RAFTERS
SPACED 16'' ON CENTERS

Timber Size	Span in Feet Eastern Spruce	Span in Feet Douglas Fir	Timber Size	Span in Feet Eastern Spruce	Span in Feet Douglas Fir
2 x 6	8	10	2 x 6	10	11
2 x 8	10	12	3 x 8	13	14
2 x 10	13	15	3 x 10	16	18
2 x 12	16	18	3 x 12	20	22
2 x 14	19	21	3 x 15	22	24

3x6 (handwritten, with circle around the "2" in "2 x 6")

NOTE: Two planks spiked together doubles the strength factor. Adding a center support more than doubles the strength. (The above specifications for roof rafters provide ample strength for normal snow loads. In mountain regions receiving extreme snow loads, use local building codes for providing additional roof support.)

This, then, is the general summary of pole construction, and the methods are the same whether you're building a chicken coop or a house.

Garden Way Associates' industrial designer, who illustrated the preceeding pages, has prepared plans of example pole buildings, which follow.

Other plans may be obtained from some of the sources listed under *References*, or, now that you have the basics in mind, you can design your own pole building.

PART FOUR

Pole
Building
Plans

Small Barn

Here in part is what Ed Robinson of the famous "Have-More" Plan wrote in 1945 about building a small barn: "Once you decide you're going to have some livestock on your place in the country, then it's obvious that you'll need a barn to house it.

"If you're primarily interested in the production of your family's food, you'll want a barn that is small, efficient, inexpensive and designed so simply that you can build it yourself if you so desire. Also, it would be a good idea to construct a barn that could be added to, or easily adapted to some other use.

"If you operate this barn at capacity it will produce more milk, eggs, chicken, lamb, squab, veal, turkey and rabbit

FINISHED SMALL BARN

Shed extension to the basic barn can be added later to the main structure, which provides for storage in the roof area.

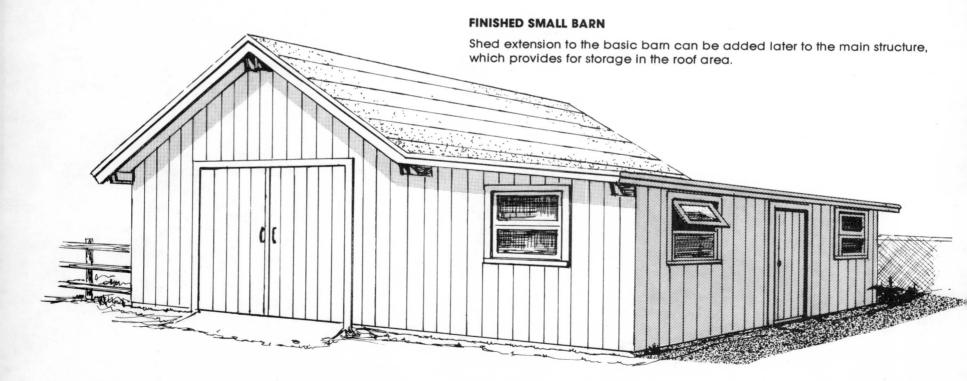

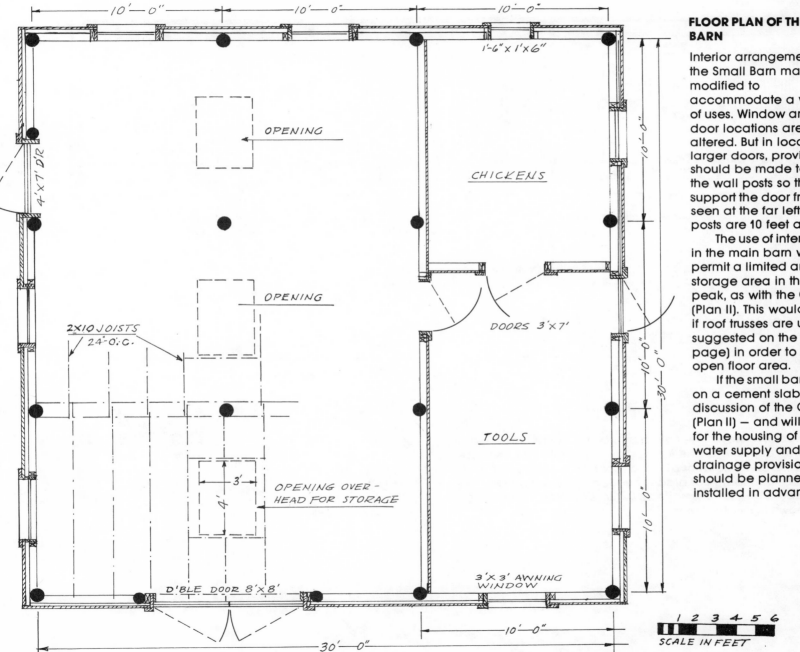

10'—0" 10'—0" 10'—0"

1'-6" X 1'-6"

OPENING

CHICKENS

4'X 7' D'R

2x10 JOISTS
24"O.C.

OPENING

DOORS 3'X7'

10'—0"

10'—0"

30'—0"

TOOLS

3'

4'

OPENING OVER-
HEAD FOR STORAGE

10'—0"

D'BLE DOOR 8'X8'

3'X 3' AWNING
WINDOW

30'—0" 10'—0"

1 2 3 4 5 6
SCALE IN FEET

FLOOR PLAN OF THE SMALL BARN

Interior arrangements of the Small Barn may be modified to accommodate a variety of uses. Window and small door locations are easily altered. But in locating larger doors, provision should be made to locate the wall posts so they will support the door frame, as seen at the far left. Other posts are 10 feet apart.

The use of interior posts in the main barn would permit a limited amount of storage area in the roof peak, as with the Garage (Plan II). This would be lost if roof trusses are used (as suggested on the next page) in order to provide open floor area.

If the small barn is built on a cement slab — see discussion of the Garage (Plan II) — and will be used for the housing of animals, water supply and drainage provisions should be planned and installed in advance.

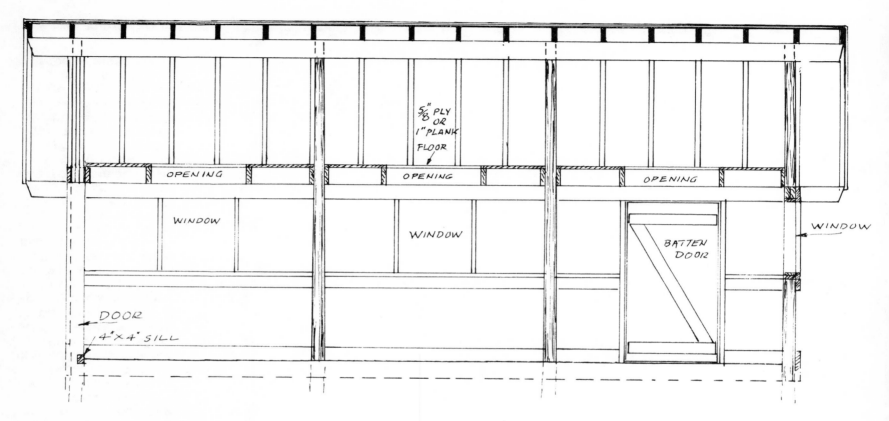

This perspective views the main barn from its center. The windows and batten door are on the far, outside wall. Note that because of the centered large door at left, a roof beam replaces the full pole there. If a clear floor area is needed in the main barn, roof trusses would be made (see Page 82) to eliminate the two interior poles shown in the floor plan.

As with the Storage Shed (Plan on Page 72) the building's siding is on the outside of the poles. Therefore, the poles are aligned so the outside faces are vertical. See also Page 42.

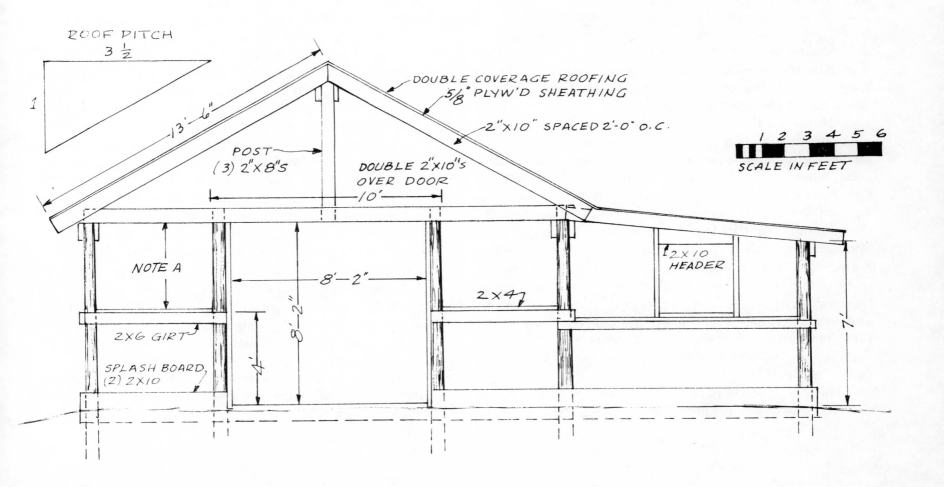

ROOF PITCH
3 ½

1

13'-6"

DOUBLE COVERAGE ROOFING
5/8" PLYW'D SHEATHING

2"X10" SPACED 2'-0" O.C.

1 2 3 4 5 6
SCALE IN FEET

POST
(3) 2"X8"S

DOUBLE 2"X10"S
OVER DOOR

10'

2 X 10
HEADER

NOTE A

8'-2"

8'-2"

2 X 4

2X6 GIRT

SPLASH BOARD
(2) 2X10

4'

7'

than a family can use. By slightly enlarging or rearranging the barn, other livestock or poultry can be added or substituted.

"Many country places already have a structure that can be made into an efficient barn. If you're in doubt as to whether or not it's better to remodel or rebuild, ask a local carpenter for an estimate both ways. If you're going to do the work yourself, pay him for his advice.

"Now, if you are figuring that you might build yourself, let me add a word of encouragement. When we moved to the country and I undertook to build my barn, I actually didn't know the first thing about how to proceed. I had had a course in manual training in grammar school and learned to saw a board and hammer a nail.

"However, I learned that there is nothing complicated about building a small barn or chicken house. If a person has just a little manual dexterity, for instance the ability to drive a car, then he should be able to build a barn with plans. Carpenters, masons, plumbers and electricians love to make a great mystery of their professions—and the building codes, the building supply people, the labor unions, the utility and applicance manufacturers do their best to keep the average householder from doing any building on his own. But the truth of the matter is that most of the skills of the average mechanic are pretty simple to master. Naturally their speed and accuracy is based on years of practice. But if you've got time, you can proceed slowly, and in the end, when your barn is done, who's to know whether it was built in a week or two months?"

The 900 square-foot 30 x 30 barn shown here will provide for the needs of all but the most ambitious home-steader. Unlike the Robinson's barn it is a pole construction. Though a section of the interior is labeled, individual demands and desires will vary, so no attempt has been made to plan it completely. The main section could be built first and the lean-to added later.

All the information needed to erect this building is contained in the earlier text. It is important to locate the site so that drainage is away from the foundation in every direction. The floor should have 8 inches of gravel under the tamped earth floor. An improvement would be a 6-inch concrete floor poured over the gravel.

The large door end of the building requires a somewhat different framing to bridge over the door. And since there is no pole in the center, a beam made of three lengths of 2 x 8s spiked together is added to support the ridge.

The doors are of the typical barn type made from vertical tongue and groove boards fastened together with battens, with at least one diagonal batten to prevent sagging. The windows are stock sizes available at lumber dealers. Establish the windows' rough opening sizes before nailing on girts, using the windows' vertical dimensions to locate the girts below the plate. Further explanation of this step will be found in the Garage Plans, Page 63.

Metal roofing can be substituted for the double coverage asphalt shown in these plans. If so, plywood roof sheathing can be omitted, although this is not recommended in cold climates, because of the insulation value and added strength provided by the plywood.

The siding used on the small Barn can be board and batten or any of the various textured plywood sidings available for exterior use.

Double Garage and Tool Shed

A choice of layouts and of roof line is possible in the construction of this building simply by moving the tool shed from the rear to either side, and by switching the location of the poles to match. In this case the distance between the poles from front to back would be 11 feet and from side to side 12½ feet.

This choice will be determined by how best the building fits on your lot, its relation to driveway and house. Note also that in the alternate version rain will drain to the sides of the building. Where the roof slopes toward the doors, a rain gutter would be indicated. In this plan the building is 28½ feet long and 25 feet wide.

Farm and country residents may wish to modify the dimensions of this building to accommodate trucks, tractors and other vehicles which require more vertical and lateral clearance than the specified 9 x 7-foot door openings, which are standard garage door dimensions. Larger overhead garage doors are available from building suppliers, though usually only on special order.

Simple modifications of these plans can be worked out to "stretch" the building both vertically and horizontally in proportions which will not materially alter the one-to-four pitch of the roof. A close calculation should be made in planning any such modifications, however, to determine the increased length needed for poles, planks, boards and sheathing to keep the needs consistent with standard lumber lengths. Bear in mind also that a lesser roof pitch might cause serious problems in snow country, while a steeper pitch might destroy the visual harmony of the building's proportions.

Prior to the start of construction of the building, additional plans should be made if there will be a need for heat in the tool shed part or the whole structure.

Except in very severe climate conditions a limited heat supply in the toolshed area may be sufficient for most needs, if that room is to contain also a workbench area. Simple insulation of the toolshed walls and roof then is indicated, as well as provision for a small space heater with roof chimney located at the blind end of the shed.

In most cases electricity for lights and power tools will be important. If the building is located near the home the wiring can be brought in by underground conduit and connected (on a new circuit) to the home's central circuit box. Make a determination ahead if there is a possibility that 220-volt service will be needed in the garage for electric heating or other heavy appliances. Otherwise the service wiring should be chosen to carry the maximum anticipated use load in the building.

It is unlikely that a water supply will be required in the garage, particularly if the building is adjacent to the home and a house sillcock is located within 50 feet. Drainage of the garage floor area may prove extremely important, however, and provisions should be made if a concrete floor is poured.

Though requiring considerable care in grading, a slab that slopes gently to a drain in its center will be the best plan because it keeps water dripping from the garaged vehicles

Garage with tool shed located at rear. Siding is textured
pl ywood or tongue and groove boards.

Alternate Arrangement of Garage locates the tool shed to the right or left of the garage doors instead of in the back.

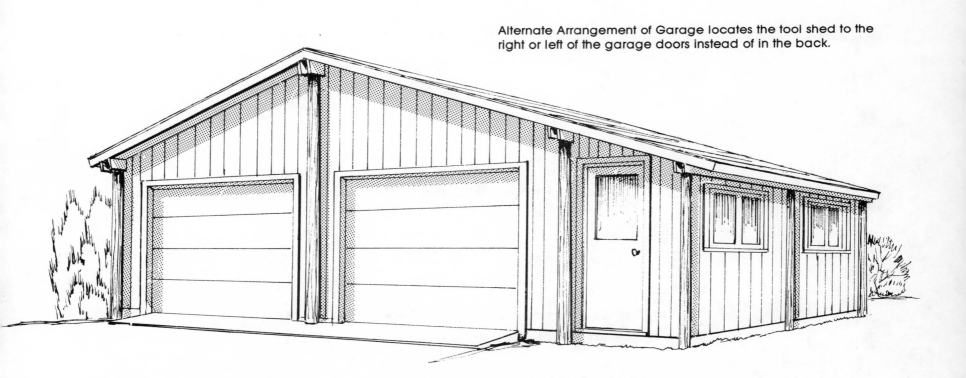

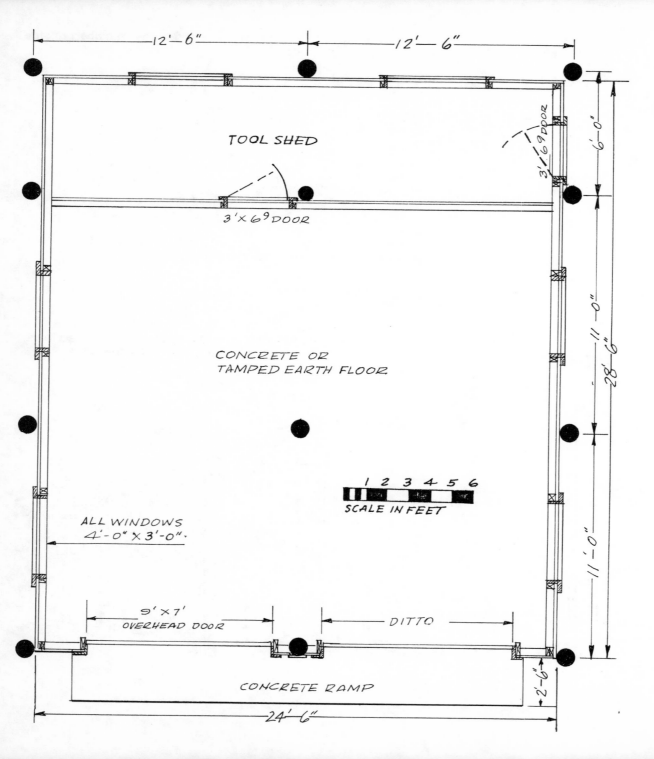

GARAGE FLOOR PLAN

Builder may decide to include a hard-surfaced floor, as discussed on Page 67.

12'-6"

12'-6"

TOOL SHED

3'-6⁹ DOOR

6'-0"

3'X6⁹DOOR

CONCRETE OR
TAMPED EARTH FLOOR

28'-6"

11'-0"

1 2 3 4 5 6
SCALE IN FEET

ALL WINDOWS
4'-0" X 3'-0".

11'-0"

9'X7'
OVERHEAD DOOR

DITTO

2'-6"

CONCRETE RAMP

24'-6"

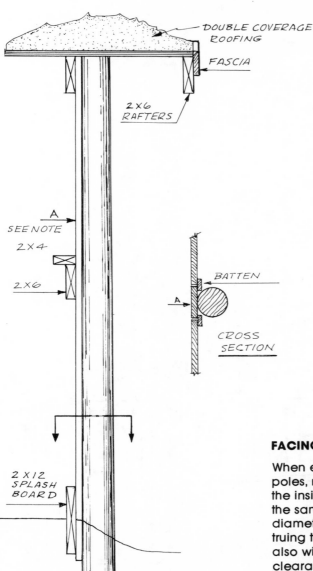

DOUBLE COVERAGE ROOFING

FASCIA

2x6 RAFTERS

A

SEE NOTE

2x4

2x6

BATTEN

A

CROSS SECTION

2x12 SPLASH BOARD

away from the building's exterior wood. Standard iron drain tiles with grill covers are available from most building supply firms.

Cement floors are prone to cracking in areas where the winters are severe, if subsoil drainage is not good and the gravel pad is not adequate. For this reason, and that it may be cheaper in some areas, a heavy blacktop floor may be a better choice, although it involves the installation by a professional paving firm. A packed earth floor may be perfectly satisfactory, however, in climates where rain and snow are not excessive.

A cement or asphalt garage floor could be added later if the earth floor proves a deterrent. It will be more difficult to do it once the building is completed, however, and the earth cover would have to be removed first from its gravel base.

FACING THE POLES

When erecting the outside poles, nail to them vertically on the inside faces, boards about the same width as the pole diameter. These will help in truing the poles vertically and also will provide the proper clearance between poles, splash board, plates and girts for the siding.

SIDE VIEW OF GARAGE

The tool shed, located at the back in this plan,
has its own access door.

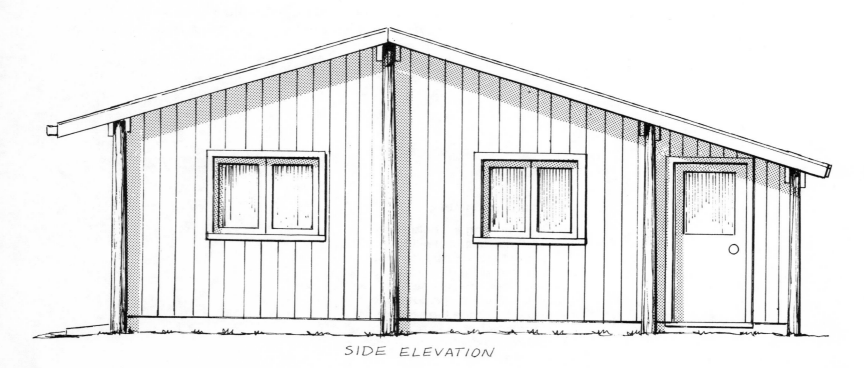

SIDE ELEVATION

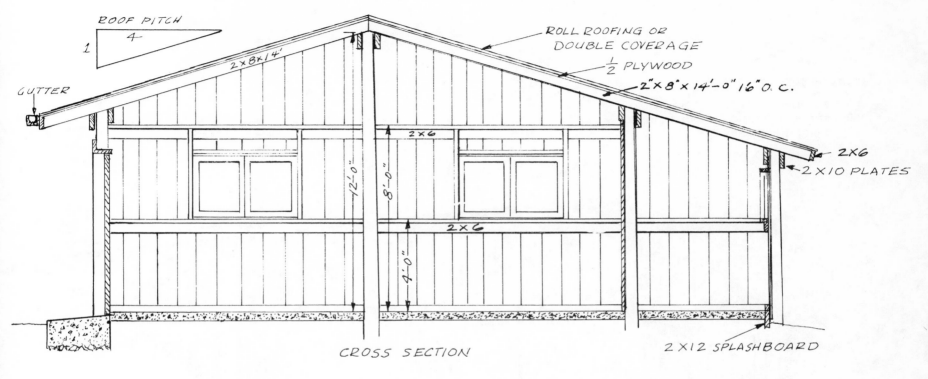

ROOF PITCH

1 / 4

GUTTER

2×8×14'

ROLL ROOFING OR
DOUBLE COVERAGE

½ PLYWOOD

2"×8"×14'-0" 16" O.C.

2×6

2×6

2×6

2×6

2×10 PLATES

12'-0"

8'-0"

4'-0"

CROSS SECTION

2×12 SPLASHBOARD

1 2 3 4 5 6

SCALE IN FEET

GARAGE CROSS-SECTION

This roof is designed to safely carry a snow
load of 40 pounds per square foot.

STORAGE SHED

In some applications this simple 7-pole building could double as housing for small animals or poultry.

Storage Shed

This 12 x 18-foot shed is designed to provide additional family storage space, as well as providing practical experience in basic pole construction. No attempt has been made to detail the design for a specific need, but it could be adapted or fitted out for housing animals or poultry kept on a smaller scale than the Stock Barn plans (Page 58) would provide for. Or the Shed might be used as a workshop of greater scope than allowed in the Garage-Tool Shed in plans on Page 63.

The poles need not be larger than 7 inches at the base for this small building, but all other directions and suggestions in the preceding text should be followed. The best roofing for this type of building considering the shallow slope is "double-coverage" roll roofing. Roughly half of each three foot strip is smooth tar-coated and the balance has a crushed mineral surface. Start at the lower side of the roof with the smooth portion of a length of the roll. (The coated half will be used to finish at the peak of the roof.) Cement this down with quick-setting asphalt cement, trimming to the roof edges. A full strip is now laid over this and nailed at the top edge in two 8 inch rows with nails 12 inches apart. Trim at edges, leaving ¼ to ⅜ inch overhang. Continue on to the peak of the roof, finishing with the balance of the first strip.

The siding can be any of several textured plywoods, such as texture 1-11, or tongue and groove siding, or the board and batten type. Windows are difficult to build, and it will be easier to buy some from a salvage building material yard or one of the various stock sizes from a lumber yard.

When locating the pole for the hinged side of the Storage Shed's door, allow a liberal distance to accommodate the door and frame. As noted on Page 37, the taper of poles often varies, and it is better to build with shims to the required doorframe width than to find the pole is too close.

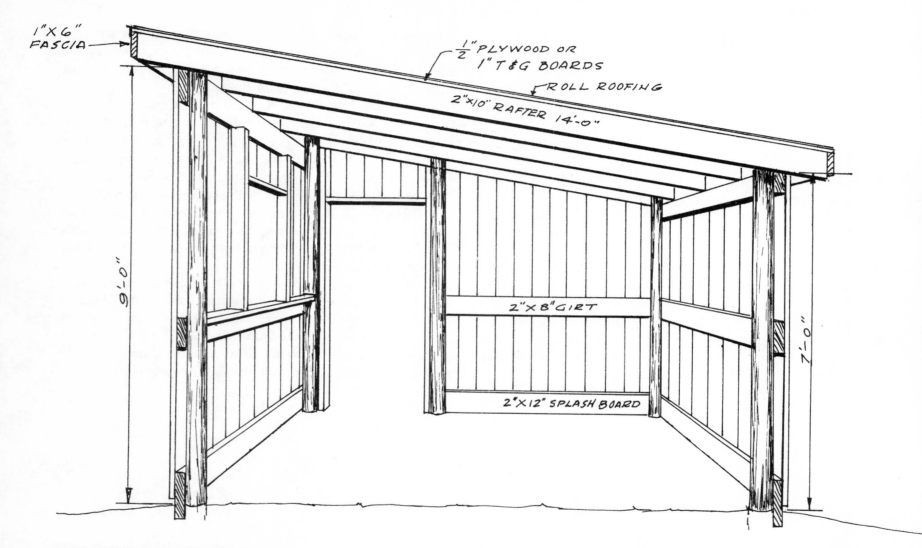

1"X6" FASCIA

½" PLYWOOD OR 1" T&G BOARDS

ROLL ROOFING

2"X10" RAFTER 14'-0"

9'-0"

7'-0"

2"X8" GIRT

2"X12" SPLASH BOARD

STORAGE SHED, CUT-AWAY VIEW

Since siding is applied to the shed pole
exteriors, the poles are aligned to keep
their outside faces vertical.

Door may be widened merely by
re-locating center pole at door edge.

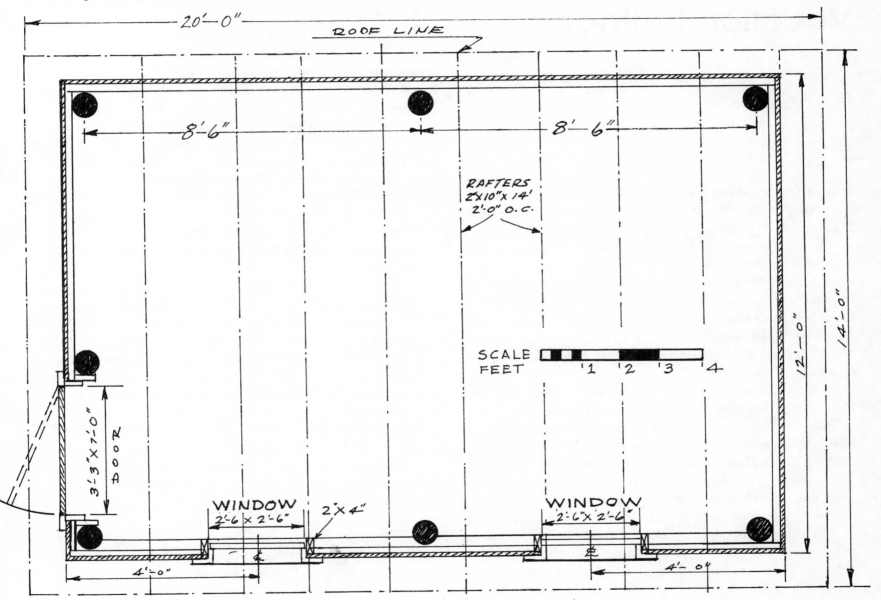

20'—0"

ROOF LINE

8'-6"

8'-6"

RAFTERS
2"x 10"x 14'
2'-0" O.C.

SCALE
FEET   '1 '2 '3 '4

12'-0"

14'-0"

3'-3"X 7'-0"
DOOR

WINDOW
2'-6" x 2'-6"

2"x 4"

WINDOW
2'-6"x 2'-6"

4'-0"

4'- 0"

Vacation Cottage

This cottage has been laid out to take advantage of standard construction lumber, which comes in increments of two feet. If you want to change the outside dimensions, keep this in mind, to avoid needless waste. In the plans it is essentially square—less the porch.

One modification of previous text instructions is very important: Because of the natural taper of poles, it is difficult to enclose them in walls. So in this and the following designs the poles are left *outside* the building proper. The poles must be set vertical to the *inside* face rather than the outside as shown on Page 42 and 67.

One of the advantages of a pole building is that none of the walls is load-bearing, so that the partitions and even outside walls can be changed at will without affecting the basic structure. The sequence of building would be: poles erected, plates attached at eaves and floor levels, followed by joists, rafters, roofing and flooring. At this stage you have a solid platform sheltered by a roof. Walls and partitions now can be constructed on this platform out of the elements.

Modifications to be considered might include eliminating the clerestory windows by raising or dropping the peak at the center line of the building, though this would diminish the ventilation and light which such windows provide.

All studding (2 x 4's) is two feet on centers to take advantage of the standard four-foot width of most plywood and panelling. Window sizes are suggested only, and accurate rough opening sizes should be checked when ordering windows. Any of various siding materials can be used, and insulation and inside finish can be added at your convenience. Refer to drawings P. 54, 85 and 87.

Like the Year 'Round Homes (plans to follow) this Vacation Cottage is sheathed on the insides of the poles. This is so that interior insulation and wall finish may be added if desired. This might be particularly useful in cold areas should the owner wish to use the cottage in the late fall or the winter. The major problem encountered then would be making provision for the portection of the water and drainage lines.

If such a conversion is a real possibility, the builder might well modify these plans to the extent of including a below-frost-line utility base, through which such water and drain lines are passed. This also would provide a solid and ready-made base for furnace and/or fireplace, should they be wanted later. Well tiles sunk below frost and brought up to floor level, if well-insulated also will provide adequate pipe protection.

Such a cold weather modification of the Vacation Cottage could be made efficiently by providing an excavated closed basement room under the bath-kitchen areas (see the Page 81 floor plans). Access to the basement room might be from outside or, more convenient for access, by providing stairs down from the porch area.

A small stove (wood or gas fired) located in this basement room would protect the water and drain pipes when in use and not drained. Floor vents would channel the heat also to the bath and kitchen areas.

VACATION COTTAGE

High and low sections of the building may be reversed, depending on its orientation to light. On this gentle slope poles rather than a keywall are used on the uphill side as shown on page 36.

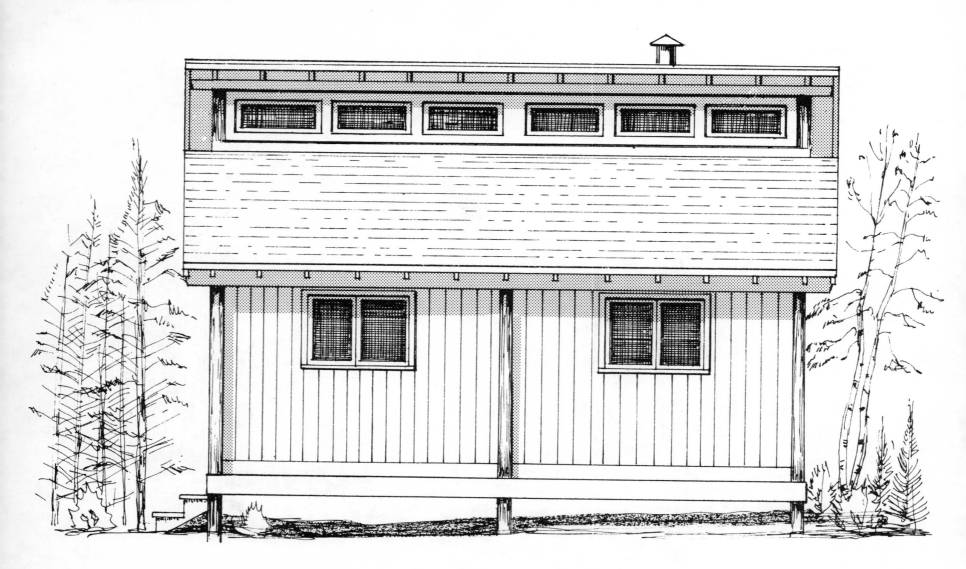

REAR VIEW OF VACATION COTTAGE

High windows between the staggered roof peaks
may be hinged to open for ventilation by remote connections.

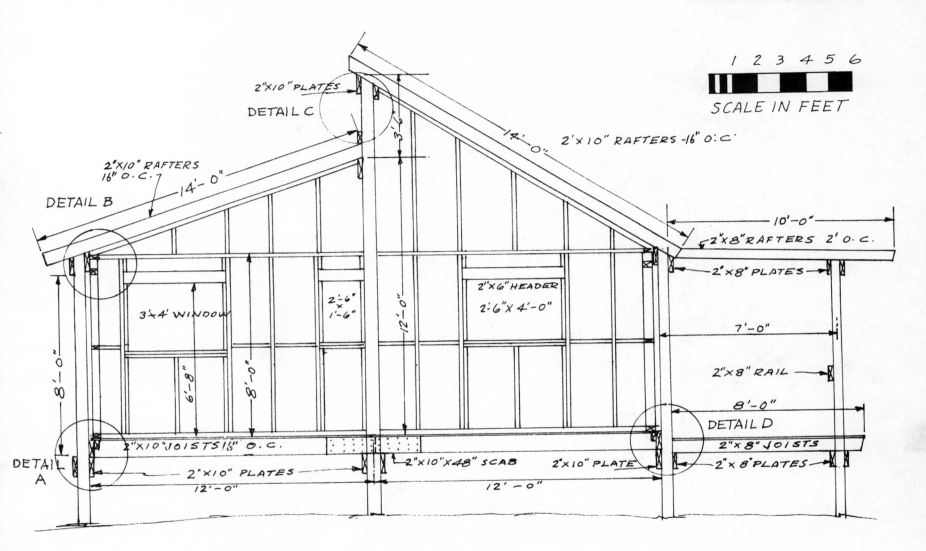

2"x10" PLATES
DETAIL C
2"x10" RAFTERS 16" O.C.
DETAIL B
2"x10" RAFTERS 16" O.C.
14'-0"
14'-0"
3'-6"
1 2 3 4 5 6
SCALE IN FEET
10'-0"
2"x8" RAFTERS 2' O.C.
2"x8" PLATES
12'-0"
2'-6" x 1'-6"
2"x6" HEADER
2'-6" x 4'-0"
3'x4' WINDOW
7'-0"
8'-0"
6'-8"
8'-0"
2"x8" RAIL
8'-0"
DETAIL D
2"x8" JOISTS
DETAIL A
2"x10" JOISTS 16" O.C.
2"x10" PLATES
12'-0"
2"x10"x48" SCAB
2"x10" PLATE
12'-0"
2"x8" PLATES

SIDEVIEW PLAN OF VACATION COTTAGE

Insulation of the cottage for off-season use would employ
application of batts under roof sheathing or, if planned for during
building, could use insulating plank sheathing as shown
on page 55.

Shown in closeup detail following are
construction details for the cottage.

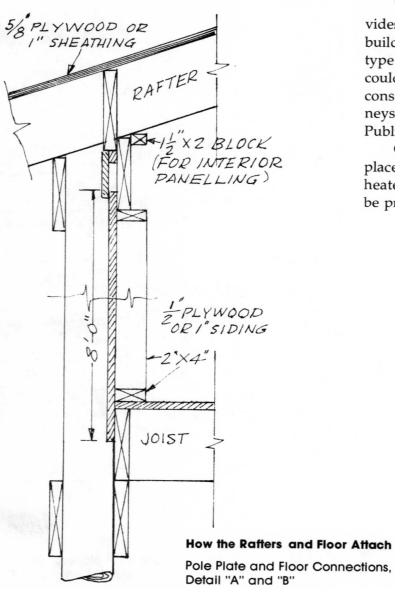

$\frac{5}{8}''$ PLYWOOD OR 1" SHEATHING

RAFTER

$1\frac{1}{2}''$ X 2 BLOCK (FOR INTERIOR PANELLING)

$\frac{1}{2}''$ PLYWOOD OR 1" SIDING

2"X4"

8'-0"

JOIST

How the Rafters and Floor Attach

Pole Plate and Floor Connections, Detail "A" and "B"

The living-dining area of the Cottage in these plans provides for a fireplace or stove, and for full winter use of the building a modern or renovated old wood stove of the parlor type could be employed. In either case a handy wood supply could be provided for by a sidewall storage box. Data on this construction as well as on lightweight, prefabricated chimneys may be found in *Wood Stove Know-How* (Garden Way Publishing.)

Grill vents in the partition wall behind the stove or fireplace will provide some welcome heat in the otherwise unheated larger bedroom. The smaller bedroom similarly can be provided with a grill vent from the bathroom if desired.

WINDOWS AT THE ROOF PEAKS, DETAIL "C"

Face-on view of the windows shows
that they are framed in outside the
poles.

Side view of the windows indicate also
arrangement of roof flashings above and
below the windows.

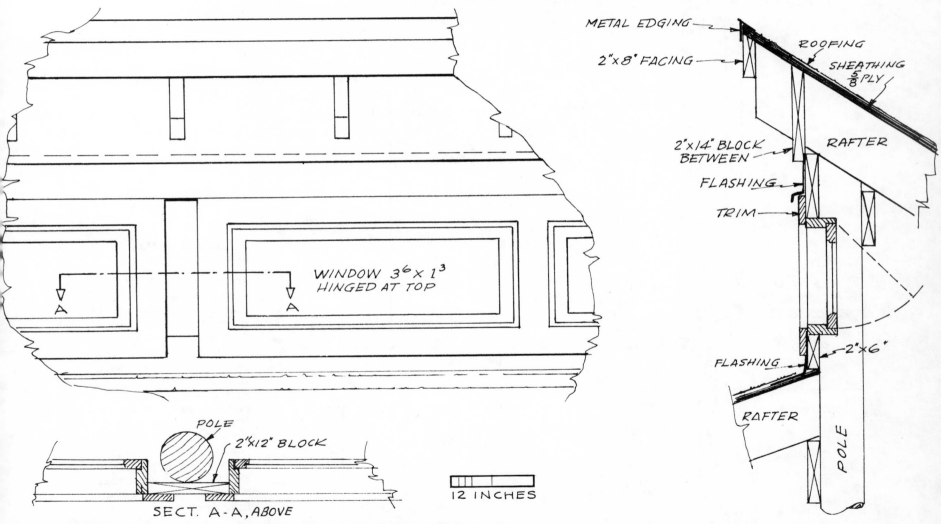

WINDOW $3^6 \times 1^3$
HINGED AT TOP

A

A

METAL EDGING

2"x8" FACING

ROOFING

SHEATHING
$\frac{5}{8}$ PLY

2"x14" BLOCK
BETWEEN

RAFTER

FLASHING

TRIM

2"x6"

FLASHING

RAFTER

POLE

POLE

2"x12" BLOCK

SECT. A-A, ABOVE

12 INCHES

This sectional view shows in detail how windows bridge around central pole.

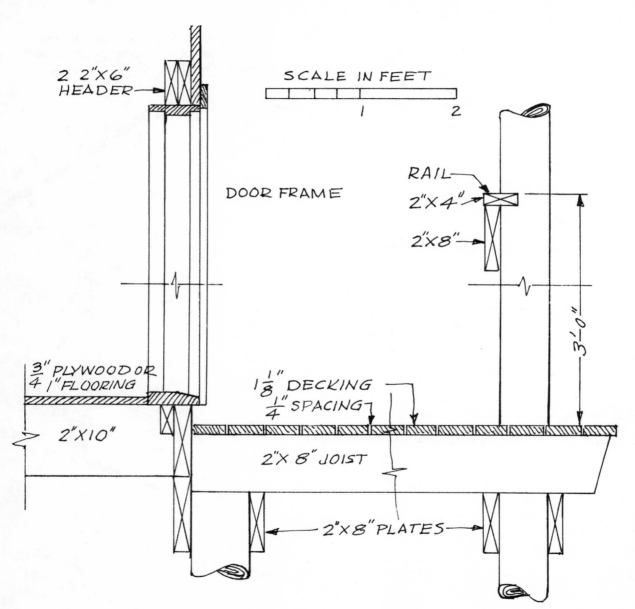

2 2"X6"
HEADER

SCALE IN FEET

1   2

DOOR FRAME

RAIL

2"X4"

2"X8"

3'-0"

3"/4" PLYWOOD OR
1" FLOORING

1 1/8" DECKING
1/4" SPACING

2"X10"

2"X 8" JOIST

2"X8" PLATES

VACATION COTTAGE PORCH

Here in Detail "D," taken from side view on page 77, is the cottage porch, hung at a slightly lower level than the main floor.

When building exterior porches or decks — such as on the Year 'Round Home, next — the use of naturally resistant woods (see Page 12) or even better the use of pressure-treated lumber for both the deck boards and floor joists will avoid much maintenance and later grief.

Bottom of this plan should face toward the cottage's best view. Top section, which houses drains, should be adjacent to terrain that is flat or slopes away. Pole distances here are 12 feet.

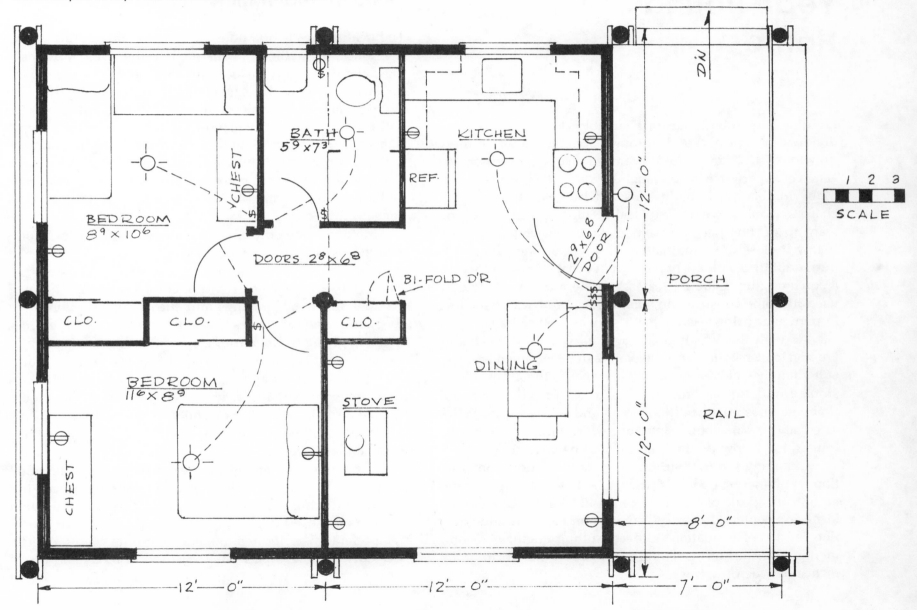

Year 'Round Home

Locating a pole building on a suitable slope can provide a dividend of a carport and a storage area, as shown in these drawings. This 28 x 40-foot house uses roof trusses to achieve a spaciousness unusual for a relatively small home. Many lumber yards build standard trusses which, if purchased, would save a great deal of time and labor. If you want to do this part yourself, make a master pattern and follow it closely, so that each truss will be the same. It is important to use plenty of nails and to coat every joint with a resorcinol glue. Glue itself has become much more widely used in home construction, the flooring and wall panelling in particular being secured with glue as well as nails.

As with the Vacation Cottage, all walls and partitions are non load-bearing, and the plans can be modified easily to suit a family's needs. A major difference is the ground floor storage and furnace room, through which all water and drainage lines must run. Bathroom and kitchen must be located above this room, and in colder climates a concrete foundation below the frost line would be advisable.

Changing the roof structure to standard pole construction involves long enough center poles to form the peak, and adding the peak plates. Rafters should be 2 x 10's sixteen inches on centers. Refer to Drawings on Pages 54 and 55 for floor and roof insulation. Our consulting engineer recommends 12 inches of insulation for floors in the North and 6 inches between the trusses.

General Heating Information

The heating needs of a house are determined by the size of the house, its method of construction, the number of openings, and its geographic location. No matter how well-built a house is or how well it is insulated there is heat loss through every surface, so any steps taken to cut down this heat loss will be worthwhile. Insulation cannot be overdone, especially in colder climates, and extra care and cost in insulating will pay for itself not only in fuel savings but in comfort.

Wind-tight skirting applied around the perimeter of buildings with elevated floors will help reduce the air flow beneath the floors.

Builders' polyethylene film for all surfaces is recommended. This comes in wide rolls and should be sandwiched between flooring, stapled to the walls after insulation is installed, and overlapped several inches. Leave the film over window and door openings and cut it to overlap onto the door and window frames. Tape or staple it to the frames before applying finished trim. All joints around the openings should be caulked with mastic applied with a calking gun.

Storm doors should be installed, and, unless the windows are made with insulating glass, storm windows should be used also. All should be carefully weatherstripped. Heavy draperies on all windows are valuable in cutting down heat losses on cold nights.

The heating system used here (and which in a modified form might be applied to the Vacation Cottage) is forced hot air, with wood, gas or oil-fired furnace located in the utility room. If oil is used the supply tank (275 or 550 gallon capacity) preferably is located outside and underground. The necessary heating capacity is measured in BTUs and it will vary according to your geographical location. The figures in

YEAR 'ROUND HOME

Utility room enclosure lies under foreground corner of the house, a carport just behind it.

the chart below represent a safe heating capacity assuming your house is well insulated. Check with your local weather bureau office for the lowest average temperature in your locality and compare with the following table.

Lowest Average Temperature	Burner Output In BTUs
−20	90,000
−10	77,500
0	69,300
+10	59,800
+20	50,300
+30	42,000

Choose a burner at or slightly above your indicated need. Too small a burner will not meet your heating needs in an unusual cold period and too large a burner will result in wasted heat and higher fuel costs.

Because of the increasing shortage and cost of oil and gas for heating purposes (we have discounted the use of electricity here for the same reasons), the builder of this home may want to look seriously into the possibilities of heating with wood, especially if he is located in an area that grows ample fuel wood supplies.

END VIEW OF YEAR 'ROUND HOUSE

Door at top of stairs enters kitchen. Living room main entrance is around corner of the deck. This also is the "view" side.

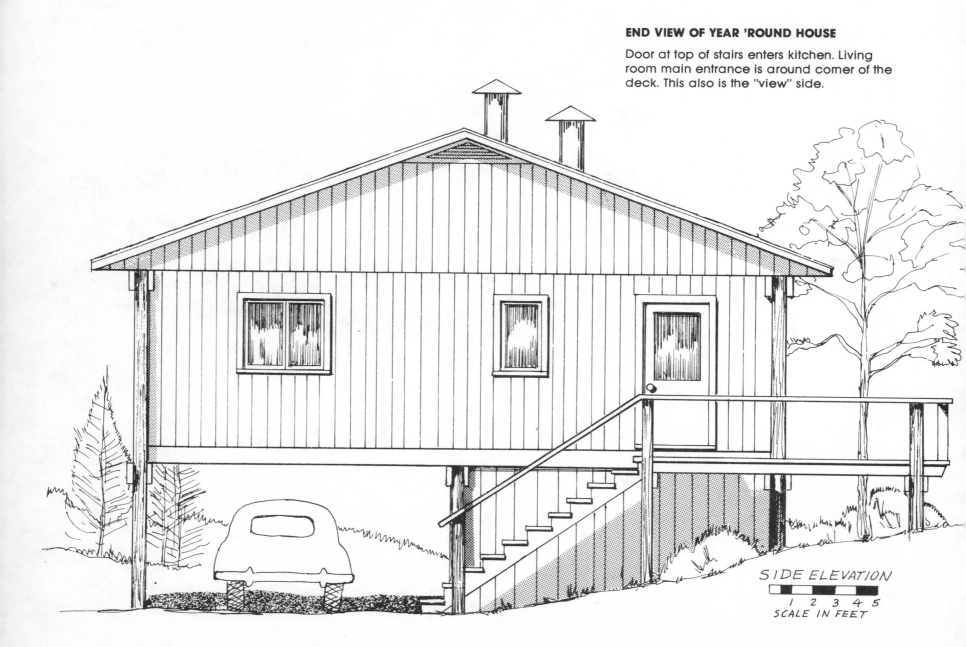

SIDE ELEVATION

1 2 3 4 5

SCALE IN FEET

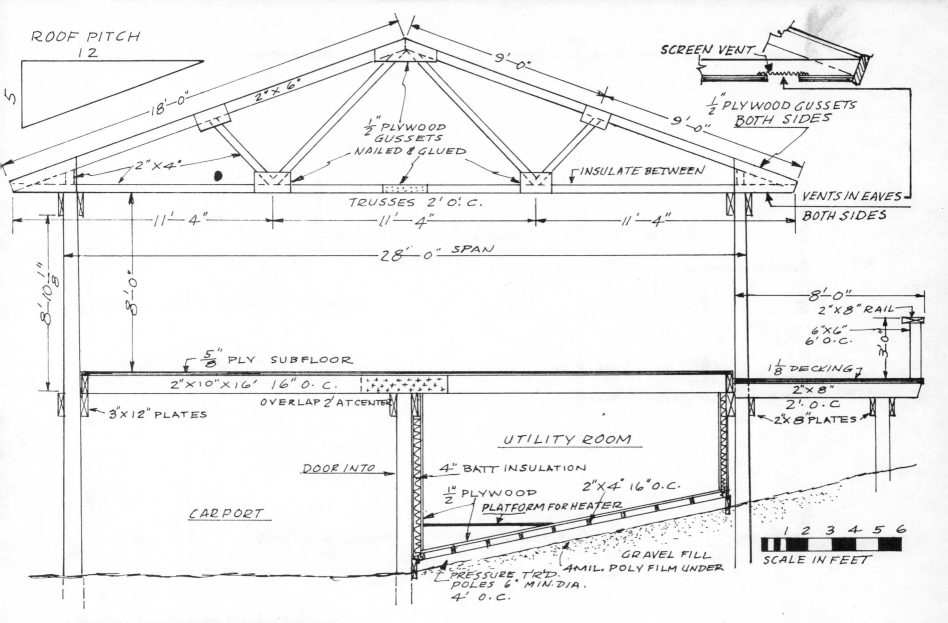

ROOF PITCH
12
5

9'-0"

SCREEN VENT

18'-0"

2"X 6"

1/2" PLYWOOD GUSSETS BOTH SIDES

9'-0"

1/2" PLYWOOD
GUSSETS
NAILED & GLUED

2"X4'

INSULATE BETWEEN

VENTS IN EAVES
BOTH SIDES

TRUSSES 2'-0". C.

11'- 4"

11'- 4"

11'- 4"

28'- 0" SPAN

8'- 0"

8'-0"

8'-10 1/8"

8'-0"

2"X8" RAIL

6"X6"
6'-0.C.

3'-0"

1 1/8 DECKING

5/8" PLY SUBFLOOR

2"X10"X16' 16" O.C.
OVERLAP 2' AT CENTER

3"X12" PLATES

2"X8"

2'-0. C.

2"X8" PLATES

UTILITY ROOM

DOOR INTO

4" BATT INSULATION

1/2" PLYWOOD

2"X4" 16" O.C.

CARPORT

PLATFORM FOR HEATER

GRAVEL FILL
4 MIL. POLY FILM UNDER

1 2 3 4 5 6
SCALE IN FEET

PRESSURE TR'D.
POLES 6" MIN. DIA.
4'-0.C.

END OF YEAR 'ROUND HOME IN CROSS-SECTION

The 28 x 40-foot ceiling area and all
the floor area (less the utility room
section) are heavily insulated for winter
comfort and fuel economy.

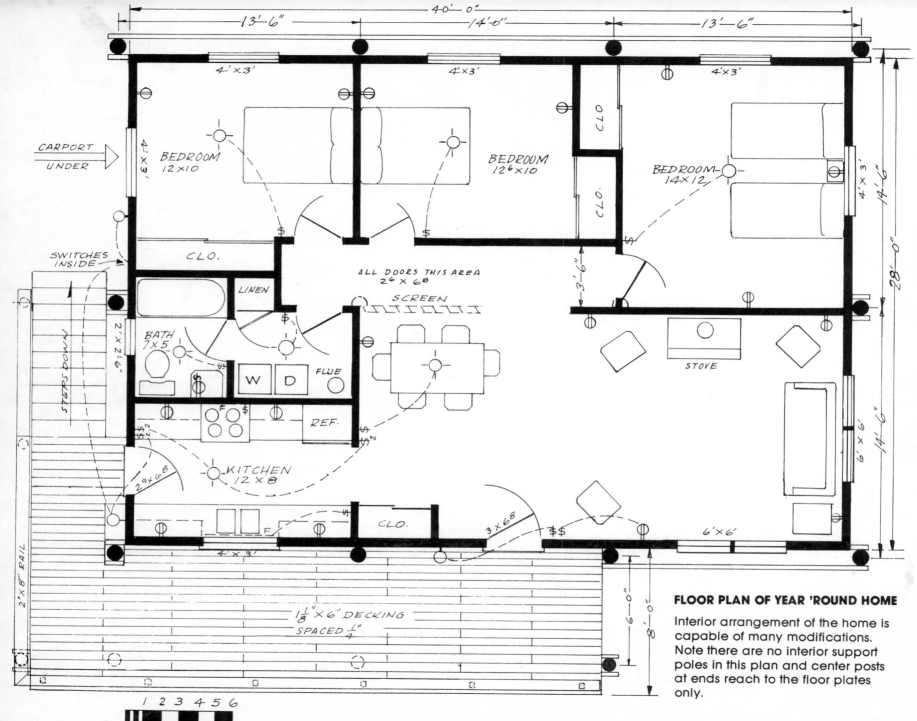

CARPORT
UNDER →

4'x3'
4'x3'
4'x3'

BEDROOM
12 x 10

CLO

BEDROOM
12⁶x10

CLO

BEDROOM
14x12

4'x3'

4'x4'

SWITCHES
INSIDE

CLO.

LINEN

ALL DOORS THIS AREA
2⁶ x 6⁸

2'x2'6"

BATH
7 x 5

SCREEN

STEPS DOWN

W   D   FLUE

3'-6"

REF.

STOVE

KITCHEN
12 x 8

2'x8" RAIL

2⁹x6⁸

CLO.

3x6⁸

6'x6'

1⅛"x6" DECKING
SPACED ¼"

4'x3'

6'x6'

6'-0"

10'-0"

8'-0"

40'-0"

13'-6"

14'-0"

13'-6"

14'-6"

14'-6"

28'-0"

1 2 3 4 5 6

SCALE IN FEET

FLOOR PLAN OF YEAR 'ROUND HOME

Interior arrangement of the home is
capable of many modifications.
Note there are no interior support
poles in this plan and center posts
at ends reach to the floor plates
only.

HEATING THE YEAR 'ROUND HOME

Since much of the floor area is open below, duct work shown here in cross-section, must be insulated carefully. Forced hot air system diagrammed here could employ part of carport area for fuel storage if a wood-fired furnace is installed.

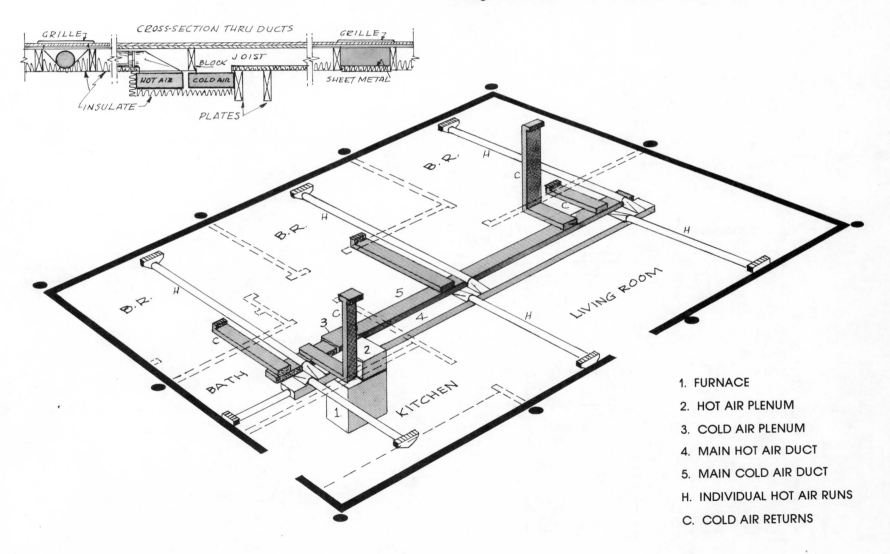

1. FURNACE

2. HOT AIR PLENUM

3. COLD AIR PLENUM

4. MAIN HOT AIR DUCT

5. MAIN COLD AIR DUCT

H. INDIVIDUAL HOT AIR RUNS

C. COLD AIR RETURNS

Heating this home with wood, however, with a modern furnace might require upwards of six cords of good, dry hardwood, depending on the severity of the area climate. This implies access to a good supply at reasonable costs, and also the construction of supplementary covered storage close to the furnace area. The user of wood for heat must be ready and able also to cope with the labor of hand stoking and ash removal at least twice daily. For further information on the manufacturers of wood furnaces see *Wood Stove Know-How* and *Heating With Wood* (Garden Way Publishing.)

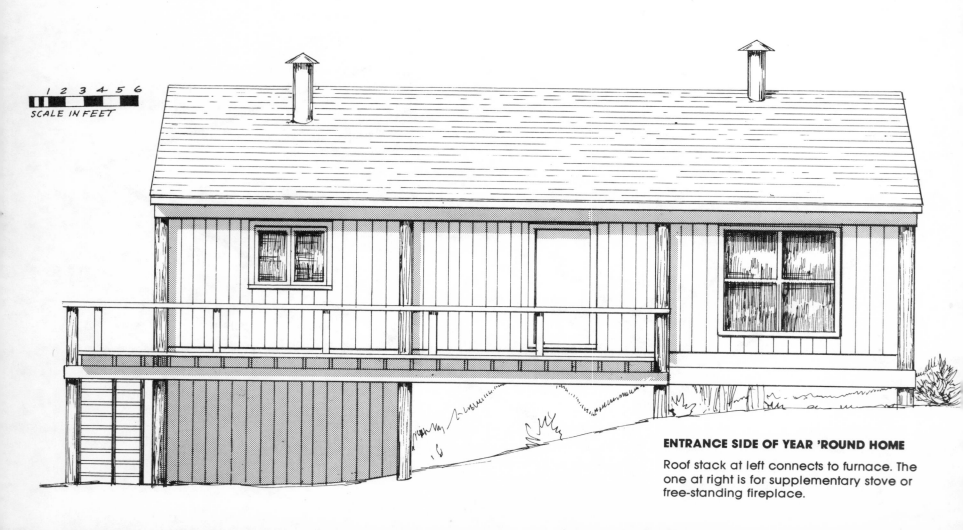

1 2 3 4 5 6
SCALE IN FEET

ENTRANCE SIDE OF YEAR 'ROUND HOME

Roof stack at left connects to furnace. The one at right is for supplementary stove or free-standing fireplace.

Of possible application here also is the combination wood and oil-fired furnace marketed by Duo-matic of Canada (Waterford, Ontario). Worth investigating in some regions, also, are coal furnaces and combination coal-oil and coal-wood heating plants manufactured by Riteway and other firms.

Finally, though the technology and equipment at this writing is not largely developed, heating of the home by the use of solar panels linked to circulated liquid radiation may be practical in sections of the country which enjoy a high ratio of sunlight hours in the winter period. Home generation of methane gas in quantities sufficient for home heating appears a very unlikely possibility except where a large cattle herd is available.

Required above the wood, gas or oil furnace are two plenums or chambers, one for the hot air feed and the other for the cold air return. From these plenums come the main rectangular ducts (8 x 16 inches.) At the appropriate places these ducts feed hot air into 6-inch diameter pipes, located between the joists, which supply hot air to each room. These ducts terminate in 90 degree boots topped with supply registers located as close as possible to the outside walls. Each of these feeder ducts should be equipped with a damper to regulate air flow.

The cold air return ducts are located in or near the interior walls and are formed by enclosing the bottom of a pair of joists with sheet metal pans, as shown in the drawing. Six-inch pipe can be used instead, if preferred, here also. The passages above the cold air ducts are blocked off with lengths of 2 x 10s. Note that the livingroom cold air duct is carried to the ceiling height between a pair of studs, while the kitchen and bath share a common cold air return. Both the hot and cold air ducts should be insulated as heavily as possible to minimize heat loss.

Electricity

How much of your own electrical work you can do is usually governed by the local building code. Some areas require that all electrical work be done by a licenced electrician while others have no code and use the standards set by the National Electric Code. Similarly some codes specify armored cable (metal-sheathed BX) while others permit the use of plastic covered Romex cable.

For the year 'round house an entrance service panel is located in the utility room with at least six branch circuits and three spares. Switches are generally located 42 inches from the floor and duplex outlets 15 inches from the floor except in the kitchen and bathroom where they should be located at a convenient height. Strip outlets against the wall over the kitchen counter are convenient for multiple use. Electric stoves and dryers need 220-volt outlets. Outdoor fixtures should be weatherproof and generally use cast aluminum lamp holders with 150 watt outdoor floodlamps. Following is an explanation of symbols used in the floor plans for the Vacation Cottage (Page 81) and two year-'round homes (Pages 86, 92 and 93):

S	SWITCH		DUPLEX OUTLET
S_2	TWO WAY SWITCH		OUTLET WITH SWITCH
	WALL FIXTURE	F	FLUORESCENT FIXTURE
	CEILING FIXTURE		CONNECTING CABLE

Split-level Home

This 36 x 38-foot year-round house, the largest and most ambitious project in these building plans, provides for 1700 square feet of living space. It is distinguished by clerestory windows in the livingroom and at the top of the stairwell. The livingroom and both upper level rooms have balconies.

A further refinement is the centrally-located utility room's concrete foundation (with cement block or poured walls), which is shown in the Cross Section (Page 95) and also in the Lower Level Floor Plan following. These two plans also show the stairway entrance to the utility room. Additional access is provided by a sliding door off the main deck (see top left area of the Floor Plan).

Plumbing and heating appliances and connections for the house are contained in the utility room and the chimney flue runs through a corner of the kitchen. A heating duct diagram is not included here, but could be planned in similar fashion to that shown with the preceeding Year 'Round Home Plan on Page 87. The use of baseboard hot water heating is recommended, however, for ease of installation.

Procedures for construction follow the main text generally. The outside poles should be trued up on their *inside* faces, following the instructions given in the caption on Page 67.

In these plans all the floor joists are connected to the plates by manufactured metal joist hangers (see Page 20), except where the upper decks or hanging balconies occur. So that these balcony joists will be cantilevered, the plates at these points are lowered the width of the joists, rather than being flush—as shown in the Balcony Detail view.

Because of the flat surfaces of the roofs, built-up gravel surfaced roofing should be planned there. Heavier than usual roof rafters and upper plates are used (see Cross Section Page 95) to allow for the extra weight of this roofing and also a possible snow load increase. Pole distances are 12 feet.

In northern climates the roof areas, as well as side walls and floors, should be heavily insulated (see General Heating Information under the plans on Page 82). The furnace for this house, when built for severe winters, should have a 160,000 BTU capacity. The electric service entrance panel, located in the utility room, should be of 200 amperes size.

Since none of the walls of the house is load-bearing, the wall studs could be located 24 inches on centers rather than the usual 16 inches. This would effect some savings in materials and in labor. The floor joists, however, should be kept at 16 inches on centers.

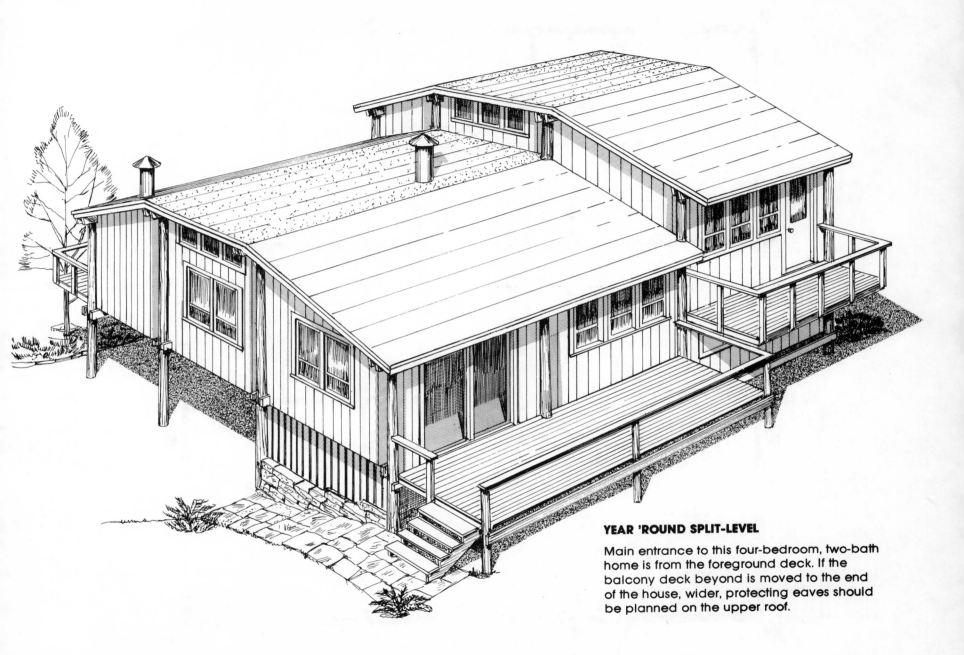

YEAR 'ROUND SPLIT-LEVEL

Main entrance to this four-bedroom, two-bath home is from the foreground deck. If the balcony deck beyond is moved to the end of the house, wider, protecting eaves should be planned on the upper roof.

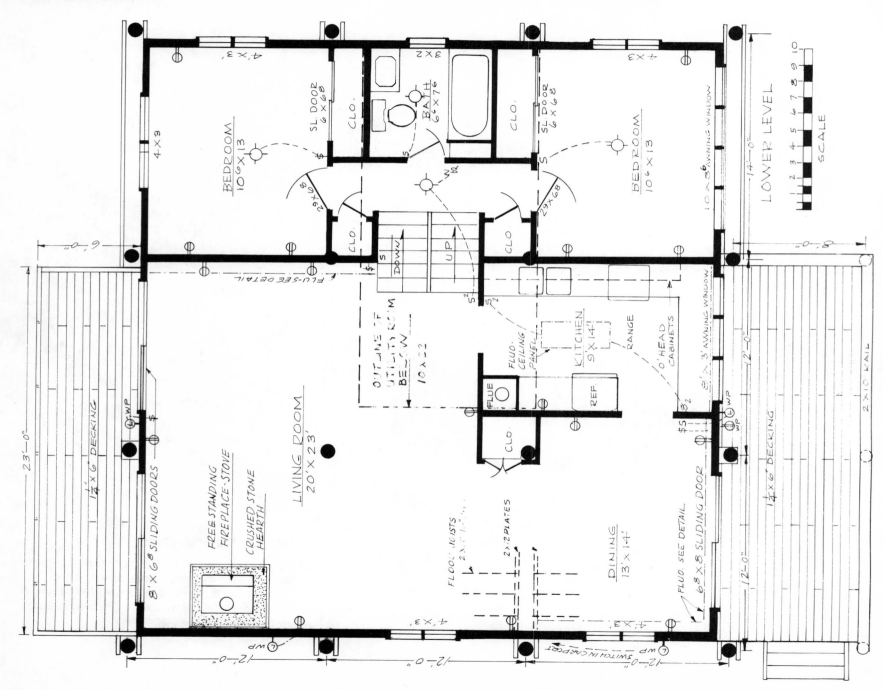

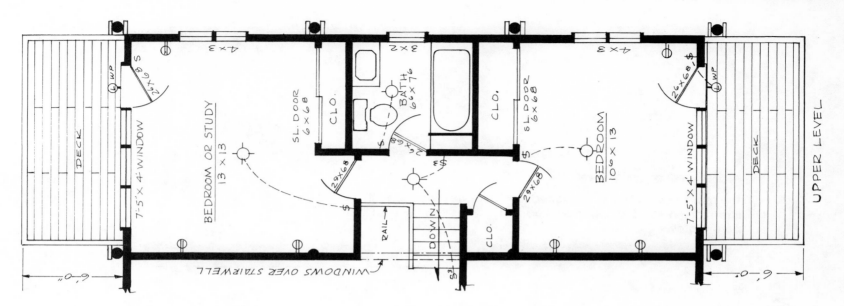

SPLIT-LEVEL FLOOR PLAN

There also is direct entrance to the home from below—from the carport area via the utility room, as shown also in Cross-Section view on Page 95. If the terrain permits, tool or fuel storage may be planned at the end of the utility room. (Turn book sideways to view these plans).

FRONT VIEW OF SPLIT-LEVEL

The main, lower deck is supported (see also view on Page 91) by three short poles. The upper level balcony hangs cantilevered from pole plates.

FRONT ELEVATION

1 2 3 4 5 6 7 8

SCALE

3'-0"

10'-0"
2×8 CANTI-
LEVER-NAIL TO
INSIDE RAFTERS
SEE DETAIL

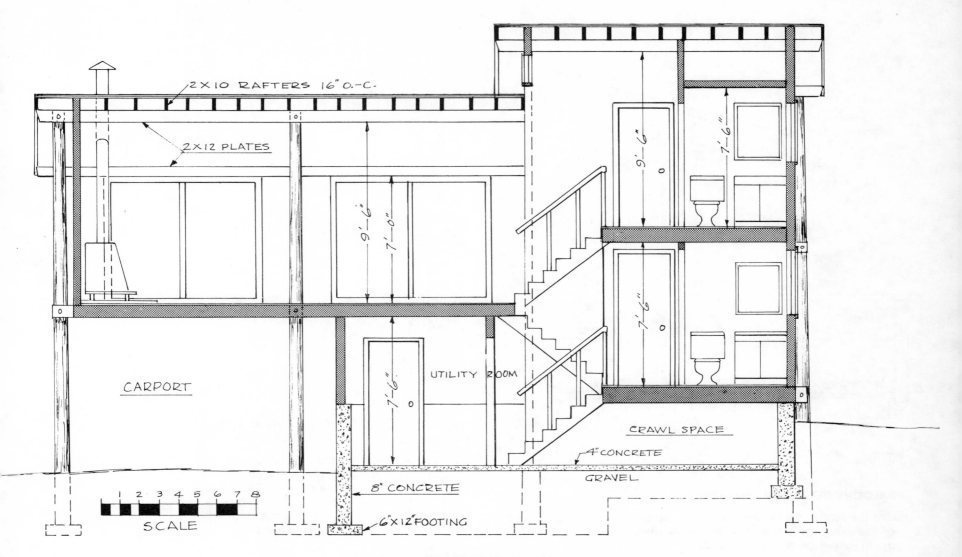

SPLIT-LEVEL CROSS-SECTION

Stairs in house center reach up to small upper hall (Page 92 Floor Plan), down to similar hall on lower sleeping level, and further down to the utility room and carport level. Carport may be entered from either end of the building.

INDIRECT LIGHTING

Standard fluorescent strips may be boxed as in this detail plan for use along an interior wall of the living room, as indicated in the Page 92 Floor Plan.

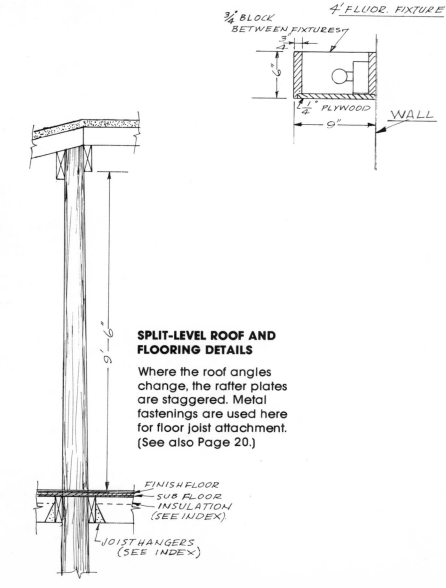

BALCONY DETAIL FOR SPLIT-LEVEL

Like the higher bedroom balconies, the deck off the living room area hangs cantilevered as an extension of the floor joists.

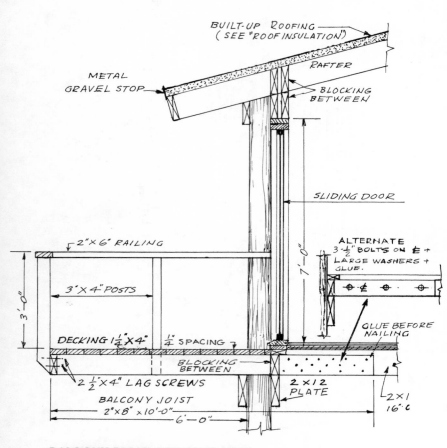

SPLIT-LEVEL ROOF AND FLOORING DETAILS

Where the roof angles change, the rafter plates are staggered. Metal fastenings are used here for floor joist attachment. (See also Page 20.)

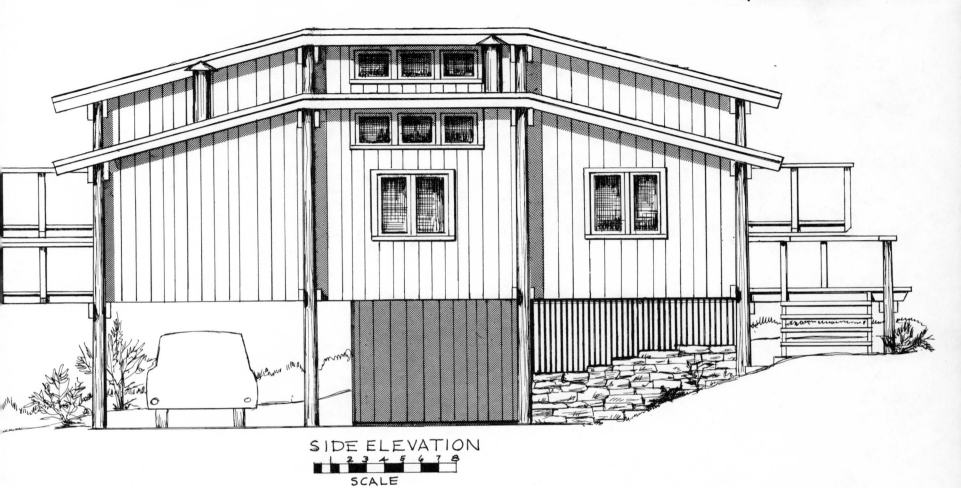

SIDE ELEVATION
1 2 3 4 5 6 7 8
SCALE

END VIEW OF SPLIT-LEVEL

Upper balconies shown here attach to the upper, corner bedrooms. The clerestory windows between the roof levels light the central stairways. The utility room at lower center is recessed 14 feet from the near wall.

ILLUSTRATIONS LIST

Suggested Tools for Pole Construction Building

hand axe
sledge hammer
carpenter's spirit level
plumb bob
carpenter's twine
carpenter's square
chalk & carpenter's pencil
claw hammer
carpenter's folding rule
reel tape measure (50 or 100 ft.)
long handled shovel
post hole shovel
block & tackle with tripod
2 adjustable wrenches
  (one long-handled if lag screws are used)
electric drill, heavy duty, ½ hp or larger
extension cord, heavy duty, 100 ft.
bits (chisel or spade type) to match lag screws or pre-bore
  for spikes or ¹/₁₆ inch larger than bolts, if used.
bit extension (1 foot) for drill
hand saw, crosscut
electric hand saw (optional)
hand chisel (1-inch) & mallet
staple gun (if batt-insulating)
keyhole saw
tin snips
caulking gun
shears (if insulating)
carpenter's apron

Bibliography

American Wood Preservers Institute, *Pole House Construction*, McLean, Va. Undated.

Anderson, L. O. & Harold F. Zornig, *Build Your Own Low-Cost Home.* Dover Publications, Inc., New York, 1972.

Cornell University, Ithaca, N.Y., Bulletin No. 401, *Pole Barn Construction.* Undated.

Kern, Ken, *The Owner-Built Home.* Oakhurst, California. 1972

Koppers Co., Inc., Pittsburgh, Penna.

Lees, Al, The Lockbox House. *Popular Science* Magazine, May, July, September, November, 1972.

Lytle, R. J., *Farm Builder's Handbook*, Structures Publishing Co., Farmington, Mich., 2nd Ed. 1973.

Oregon State University Cooperative Extension Service, *Pole Type Structures.* 1968.

Patterson, Donald, *Pole Building Design.* American Wood Preservers Inst., McLean, Va. 1969.

Rapoport, Amos, *House Form and Culture.* Prentice Hall, Inc., Englewood Cliffs, N.J. 1969.

Roberts, Rex, *Your Engineered House.* M. Evans & Co., New York. 1964.

Southern Forest Products Ass'n., *How to Build Pole Type Frame Buildings.* New Orleans, La. Undated.

Norum, W. A., *Pole Buildings Go Modern.* Proceedings of the American Society of Civil Engineers, Journal of the Structural Division, April 1967.

Teco, 5530 Wisconsin Ave., Washington, D.C. 20015

Index